Fountainhead of Federalism

HEINRYCHVS BVLLINGERVS
GVNDECIMI IAM NVNC LABVNTVR SYDERA LVSTRI,
HÆC ÆTAS, FORMAM PICTA TABELLA REFERT
NIL EGO VEL FORMAM VEL VITÆ TEMPORA SPECTO,
SED CHRISTVM, VITÆ QVI MIHI FORMA MEÆ EST.

FOUNTAINHEAD OF FEDERALISM

Heinrich Bullinger
and the Covenantal Tradition

Charles S. McCoy
and J. Wayne Baker

With a Translation of

De testamento seu foedere Dei unico et aeterno (1534)

by Heinrich Bullinger

Westminster/John Knox Press
Louisville, Kentucky

© 1991 Charles S. McCoy and J. Wayne Baker

Heinrich Bullinger's portrait is reproduced courtesy the Zentralbibliothek Zürich, Graphische Sammlung.

The photograph of the original title page of *De testamento seu foedere Dei unico et aeterno* is reproduced courtesy the Bienecke Rare Book and Manuscript Library, Yale University.

Book design by Gene Harris

First edition

Published by Westminster/John Knox Press
Louisville, Kentucky

PRINTED IN THE UNITED STATES OF AMERICA

9 8 7 6 5 4 3 2 1

Library of Congress Cataloging-in-Publication Data

McCoy, Charles S.
  Fountainhead of federalism : Heinrich Bullinger and the covenantal tradition / Charles S. McCoy and J. Wayne Baker ; with a translation of De testamento seu foedere Dei unico et aeterno, 1534, by Heinrich Bullinger. — 1st ed.
      p.   cm.
  Includes bibliographical references and indexes.
  ISBN 0-664-21938-1

  1. Covenant theology—History of doctrines—16th century.
2. Covenant theology—Early works to 1800. 3. Reformed Church—
History of doctrines—16th century. 4. Reformed Church—Early
works to 1800. 5. Bullinger, Heinrich, 1504–1575. 6. Federal
government. 7. Federal government—United States. I. Baker, J.
Wayne. II. Bullinger, Heinrich, 1504–1575. De testamento seu
foedere Dei unico et aeterno. English. 1991. III. Title.
BT155.M33 1991
231.7'6—dc20   91-3483

Contents

Introduction

Federal theology and political philosophy are central in the shaping of the society and the institutions of modern Western nations. They are no less crucial for an understanding of the Reformed tradition of the Christian faith. While their importance is clear, it is also unhappily the case that the history and the nature of federalism are not well known among theological scholars, even those of the Reformed churches, or among political philosophers and historians. The efforts of persons like Gottlob Schrenk in Europe and Carl J. Friedrich and Perry Miller in the United States to recover the federal tradition are impressive, but their work has not led to a general renewal either of acquaintance with or appraisal of the powerful stream of federal thought that has been the core, for good or ill, of what can be called the modern world.

In one way, the problem can be seen as a strange case of amnesia. The Chicago historian Ralph Ketcham, for example, published an article in 1958 in which he explored the origin of Madison's understanding of human nature.[1] He inquired whether the source of Madison's views might be Locke, Hobbes, Montesquieu, Bodin, or some other European thinker. Convinced that none of these had views closely congruent with Madison's, he turned to the ancient world—Aristotle, Plato, Thucydides, and Herodotus, rejecting each as differing from Madison. The conclusion that he drew at the end of the article was that we simply do not know the source of Madison's views on this important issue. In this article, Ketcham does not explore or even entertain the possibility that Madison might have derived his understanding of human nature from the federal tradition embedded in the colonial institutions and experience surrounding Madison and exemplified in John

7

Witherspoon, who taught Madison theology and political philosophy at Princeton. Ketcham appears to be unaware that such
a tradition exists. It is as though he has a case of amnesia, so that
he overlooks the obvious.

In the case of certain other scholars, the problem appears to
derive from what we may call national myopia. For example,
writing about the strengths and weaknesses of the Westminster
Confession, James B. Torrance, professor of systematic theology in the University of Aberdeen, writes:

> The Westminster Confession enshrines the "federal scheme,"
> and is the first post-Reformation confession to do so. It is beyond
> the scope of this paper to elaborate. But the issue is one of
> enormous importance, because federal theology, which first
> developed among the Puritans of England, came into Scotland
> about 1596 under Robert Rollock, and soon became the absolute
> criterion of orthodoxy and was equated with "Calvinism." The
> basic concept is that of *foedus* ("covenant" or "contract").[2]

Whether myopia, amnesia, or inadequate scholarship, there is
no excuse for the errors in this paragraph. The resources are
certainly available in contemporary works by German and
American scholars, even articles in encyclopedias written in
English if one does not read German or lacks the time to read
lengthy books by foreign authors, to provide enough information to correct some of the misstatements. The federal theology
did not originate among the Puritans of England, though there
were powerful spokespersons in England for federalism. A
more accurate understanding of the federal tradition would
make it impossible to say that it became the criterion of
orthodoxy in the Reformed churches or was equated with
Calvinism. Torrance's misunderstanding of federal theology
leads him in the article to serious distortions of its significance
in the context of the Westminster Assembly and its impact on
Reformed thought.

Yet another explanation may be possible for the general lack
of knowledge about the federal tradition. Rather than attrib-
uting the lack primarily to amnesia or to inadequate and
myopic scholarship, helpful as these explanations may be, it is
perhaps the case that human covenants and federal perspectives occupy so central and pervasive a place in the experience
and action of persons in contemporary Western societies that
federalism has become invisible to those who dwell in our
covenantal culture. People who wear spectacles do not look at
the glasses but see everything through them. In the same way,
perhaps, persons for whom Western culture is their native

habitat may not see the covenantal character of their communities simply because they see everything through their federal spectacles. As someone has remarked, whoever it was that discovered water, we may be sure it was not the fish who dwell in it as the medium of their existence. This book is an attempt to help historians, political philosophers, theologians, and ordinary church people and citizens to overcome whatever it is that blocks out an understanding of this movement which is so important for understanding our history, our society, and our own existence. As the federal tradition comes back into view, its basic ideas about human nature will be a surprise to those brought up on the curiously mistaken notion that Western societies are founded on liberal individualism. Johannes Althusius, the first systematic expositor of federal political philosophy and one whose thought has pervasive direct and indirect influence on European and American political orders, understands humans as existing only in symbiotic relationship. He speaks of humans not as individuals but rather as *symbiotes*. It may come as new information to some that government based on covenant or compact was thoroughly embedded in the federal tradition prior to Hobbes and Locke, who probably may best be regarded as later variants of federal thought. And not everyone may be aware that federalism had well-articulated notions of the division of powers and their limitation through checks and balances before Montesquieu formulated them so well that federalists quoted him to bolster convictions they already held, not to attribute their origin to him.

In this volume we include the treatise *The One and Eternal Testament or Covenant of God,* a translation of Heinrich Bullinger's *De testamento seu foedere Dei unico et aeterno.* This treatise has never been published in English. But it is the first work that organizes the understanding of God, creation, humanity, human history, and society around the covenant. It must be regarded therefore as the point of origin or the fountainhead of federalism as it has increasingly come to permeate the world in the four and one half centuries since its publication.

The introductory essay has been written in order to provide better understanding of this work and to delineate the development of the federal tradition that finds its beginning in Bullinger's work. These brief chapters are not intended to be definitive but only suggestive of the importance and potential of this area for further study. We include a section on Bullinger himself, the circumstances that gave rise to the treatise, and a brief summary of its main points; sections on the development of federal theology and political philosophy; and a short account of the people and the movements through which federalism became pervasive in Western society.

In order to make this account of the development of federalism useful in many academic disciplines and to persons in various political and ecclesiastical positions, we have tried to avoid technical terminology. Instead, we have sought to lower the barriers of language and different cultural perspectives so that the federal shaping of the modern world can be seen clearly. That is the reason, for example, that we use the word "federalism" to describe the beginning as well as the developed form of this theological-political movement.

Finally, we have assembled a moderately comprehensive bibliography on the federal tradition. It will be useful both to scholars specializing in this period and to those less well acquainted with federalism who wish to study it further.

We wish to express our appreciation to many persons who have assisted at various stages along the way toward the completion of the manuscript. Richard Leliart and Marsha McCoy helped with the translation. Michael McGiffert provided helpful suggestions. Audrey Englert contributed her secretarial skill at the word processor in providing the successive drafts. Our thanks to these and others.

Fountainhead of Federalism

Part One

1

Heinrich Bullinger
and the Origins
of the Federal Tradition

When we seek the origins of a movement as widespread and pervasive in modern society as federalism, the task of tracing the varied lines of development is obviously difficult and subject to many difficulties of interpretation. The relation of political federalism to covenantal thought in religious and theological traditions is one problem. The generalized influences from ancient and medieval sources must also be considered. The varied manifestations of federalism can raise questions about the precise criteria for identifying what should and should not be included under this heading. Much more research must be carried out in order to resolve these problems. In the meantime, our investigations have led us to Zurich as the place where diverse influences came to focus and produced a movement and a pattern of thought that can be identified as federal. The first treatise to be focused thematically on the covenant and contain political and theological views that are explicitly federal is Heinrich Bullinger's *De testamento seu foedere Dei unico et aeterno*, published in 1534. In the light of the impact of this work and the federal perspective of Bullinger, we believe that it is accurate to speak of this treatise as the fountainhead of federalism.

What Is Federalism?

Before we go farther, it will be helpful to clarify the meaning of federalism and its background. These brief discussions are not intended to be definitive but to provide orientation to federalism in its mature expression and historical setting.

First, the terms "federal" and "covenantal" are closely related and, when carefully examined, virtually interchangeable. "Federal" derives from the Latin *foedus,* which means covenant. A covenantal order is federal. A federal order is covenantal.

Academic specialization has separated federal and covenantal. Political thought has appropriated federalism as applicable to certain political patterns of the modern world. Biblical studies and theology have kept the word "covenant," understanding it as a concept prominent in the Bible and a topic in Reformation and post-Reformation Christian doctrine. What has been forgotten as academic disciplines have tended to isolate themselves from one another is that federal terminology is used by theological and political writers, as also is the language of covenant, compact, and contract. In the sixteenth, seventeenth, and eighteenth centuries, the era when the institutions of the modern world were taking shape, federal theologians dealt with political as well as ecclesiastical issues and political philosophers concerned with societal covenants dealt also with religious issues. Heinrich Bullinger and Samuel Rutherford were primarily religious leaders but did not hesitate to spell out the political implications of their theological federalism. On the other hand, political thinkers like Johannes Althusius and Thomas Hobbes focused on the political order but included much that now would be regarded as in the domain of theology. All four are deeply immersed in the covenantal or federal tradition.

We speak of Bullinger's 1534 treatise, *The One and Eternal Testament or Covenant of God,* as the fountainhead of federalism. By that, we mean that it is a basic source of federal thought among theologians, political philosophers, and practicing leaders in church and state. This influence was direct in the century following its publication and indirect during later times.

Second, federalism understands the relationships between God and the world and among humans as based on covenants among their members, some tacit and inherited from the past, others explicit and made or renewed in the present. As Carl Friedrich has put it, "A federal order typically preserves the institutional and behavioral features of a *foedus,* a compact between equals to act jointly on specific issues of general policy."[1]

In the Bible, humans make covenants with one another that shape economic, political, and familial relations. The relation of God with the creation and with humanity is depicted in covenantal terms. God makes a covenant with Noah, all humanity, and nature after the flood, with Abraham and his descendants, and with the Hebrew people after the deliverance from bondage in Egypt. Federal theologians affirm that God's covenant originally is with nature and with all humans in creation and that subsequent covenants continue, renew, and respond to the compact by which the world was created. Federal political philosophers, in varied ways, affirm this pattern. For example, Hobbes, as he made clear in the introduction to *Leviathan,* understood the state as created by human compact in a way parallel to God's covenantal fiat creating the world. Some federal thinkers understand the relations within the Godhead among the persons of the Trinity as based on social, federal or covenantal relations.[2] In federal perspective, the most fundamental affirmation about God for Christians is that God is the faithful One, who makes covenant and keeps covenant.

Third, the inner nature of social groups and the relationships among them are understood as covenantal by federalists. Primary social entities such as families, congregations, occupational guilds, and commercial organizations exist by virtue of the tacit and explicit compacts defining relations among members and committing participants to the group. More comprehensive social structures are based on compacts among less inclusive groups. In political organization, a town is made up of a compact among families, a province of a compact among towns, a commonwealth of a compact among provinces, and international relations of compacts among commonwealths. Church organizations and commercial associations usually exemplify this federal pattern, so it is not exclusively political in the sense of being applicable only to governmental organizations. The elements of voluntary participation, of the rights and responsibilities of membership, of commitment to the group and its patterns of governance, and of holding leaders to their covenanted obligations are central to a federal order whether ecclesiastical, economic, or political.

Fourth, federalism emphasizes division of powers within every level of organization and among these levels. The checks and balances against excessive concentration and misuse of power follow from this division, though functional efficiency and appropriateness of action is also a reason for it. This aspect of a federal order has become so widely practiced and observed that the understanding of federalism is often defined in terms only of these two elements, at the expense of a broader, more accurate view.

Fifth, it is important to view "federalism and federal relations in dynamic terms," as Friedrich reminds us. Rather than a static pattern or design, he explains, federalism is "primarily the process of federalizing a political community, that is to say, the process by which a number of separate political communities enter into arrangements for working out solutions, adopting joint policies, and making joint decisions on joint problems, and conversely also the process by which a unitary political community becomes differentiated into a federally organized whole. Federal relations are fluctuating relations in the very nature of things. Any federally organized community must therefore provide itself with instrumentalities for the recurrent revision of its pattern of design."[3]

In federal theology this dynamic element is affirmed by viewing the creation of the world and humanity, not as complete, but as developing toward ever greater fulfillment within the unfolding economies of the covenant of God. God's covenant is not a static order but a pattern of changing relations in the world toward greater justice and love.

Sixth, federalism, either tacitly or explicitly, holds views of human nature and history. Both humanity and history are understood developmentally, as moving toward fulfillment, and humans are understood as social and covenantally shaped and committed. The mix of good and evil in history and the compound of original goodness and fallen sinfulness in human nature eliminates the possibility of an easy optimism or a notion of automatic progress with reference to the future. Yet there is, among federalists from Bullinger to Johannes Althusius, John Winthrop, and James Madison, a strong element of hope within republics shaped for the federal perspective.

Federalism: Historical Setting

There was no single background to federalism in the centuries prior to the Reformation. There were, however, several possible sources that may have helped to inspire the idea: intellectual-theological, ecclesiastical, and political precedents.

Among the sources of the federal political tradition, one that cannot be ignored is the ancient Semitic society whose history and stories were recorded in the Jewish and Christian Scriptures. According to the Bible, the covenant described the relation of God to the entire created order, was a way for understanding human nature and history, and provided the pattern of organization of society. Though a kind of federal organization may be said to have existed among the Greeks in the Athenian confederacy of city-states, it is significant that neither Plato nor Aristotle mentioned anything like a federal political philosophy.

Bullinger drew heavily on the Bible and used several church

fathers to give his idea of the covenant a past, in order to demonstrate that it was not an innovation but the very fabric from which the history of salvation was woven through the centuries, from Adam to his own day. He cited Augustine, Irenaeus, Tertullian, Lactantius, and Eusebius for patristic support. Augustine and Eusebius fully supported Bullinger's idea of the unity of the people of God throughout history, but neither of them held to Bullinger's concept of the covenant. Irenaeus was the only church father who hinted at a conditional covenant, and he may well have influenced the formation of Bullinger's covenantal idea.[4]

Late-medieval nominalism was another possible source for the Reformed idea of the covenant. Heiko Oberman writes of

> an emerging new image of God. . . . God is a covenant God, his *pactum* or *foedus* is his self-commitment to become the contractual partner in creation and salvation. . . . In the nominalist view man has become the appointed representative and partner of God, responsible for his own life, society and world, on the basis of and within the limits of the treaty or *pactum* stipulated by God.[5]

In the nominalist view, the covenant between God and humans was thus bilateral or conditional.

While the nominalist idea of *pactum* was certainly pervasive in the early sixteenth century, it is unlikely that it had any crucial influence on the formulation and development of the Reformed concept of the covenant in Zurich. First, as Oberman notes, the nominalist "pact" found its basis in a Pelagian doctrine of justification, to which Bullinger could not have subscribed. Second, Bullinger was educated in the *via antiqua*, not in the nominalist *via moderna*. It is unlikely, then, that he was directly influenced by the nominalist idea of "pact." Still, the idea, current in his day, may have suggested to him the notion of a conditional covenant, which he developed within the general parameters of the Reformation theology of grace. Medieval theology thus had only a minimal influence on the Reformed doctrine of the covenant. Impetus for the rise of explicitly federal thought in the sixteenth century came from several sources. First, the organization of the Germanic tribes that invaded and settled western Europe was covenantal or federal in structure. These social patterns were continued in the covenants that underlay feudalism, in such pacts as those represented in the defensive and commercial covenants of the Hanseatic League and in political orders like the Swiss Confederation. The most direct impact from the Middle Ages on the development of the Reformed, modern idea of federalism came from the manner in which society and the church were organized in the late Middle Ages. The spirit of association can be found on several levels in the period. On the ecclesiastical level, memories of parliaments and estates-generals led to the conciliarist argument that the papacy was a limited monarchy, subject to the representative council of the church. On the economic level, the guild system is the most obvious example. More directly, however, the federation of north German towns known as the Hanseatic League is an excellent example of federalism during the medieval period. It referred to itself as a *confederatio.* While it was essentially a league for trade purposes only, the idea of a confederation also had political possibilities.

The clearest example of political federalism in the medieval period is the Swiss Confederation, formed in 1291. Zurich had become a member of the Confederation in 1351. Bullinger thought about the passage in Genesis in which God made the covenant with Abraham and about Paul's comments on this covenant in Galatians, and it brought to mind the confederation in which he lived. In 1528, just at the time when he was developing his theological concept of the covenant, he published his *Admonition,* in which he urged a reformation of the entire Confederation. Here he clearly connected the biblical covenant with the political federation when he wrote, acting the part of the prophet and paraphrasing God, "Dear Confederates, remember now that in baptism you have bound yourselves to me with an oath stronger than the one with which you have bound one state to another among yourselves." The Confederates must abandon their apostasy, and "serve me with faith, love and innocence."[6]

The renewed attention to the Bible at the time of the Renaissance and the Reformation and to the covenantal social order depicted there found an especially favorable context in Switzerland. It is no accident that a specifically federal tradition finds its fountainhead in Zurich and that an explicitly federal political philosophy takes shape and emerges within the environment provided by the Reformed communities in Europe and America. Within these communities, in particular the United Provinces of the Netherlands as well as Switzerland, there was not only thought and writing about federalism but also the practice of federal politics. It was probably inevitable that federal political philosophy would be formulated in this situation in which all of human life and, indeed, the entire creation were seen in covenantal perspective.

The medieval background to the Reformed idea of the covenant was thus diverse. One might say that the idea was in the air: the nominalist theology of "pact"; the conciliar spirit of association; the economic confederations; and the political federalism of the Swiss Confederation. All that was necessary to make possible the development of the modern concept of federalism was the new emphasis on the Bible during the Reformation. When Reformed leaders read the Bible, they were reminded of something that had been part of everyday life for the forebears and for them. The result was the theological idea of the covenant, which differed from the nominalist "pact" because it was cast within the framework of the new Reformation theology of grace, and the modern political idea of federalism, which grew out of theological federalism. Heinrich Bullinger of Zurich brings these varied elements together in work that can with justice be regarded as the fountainhead of federalism.

Bullinger: Life and Work

Heinrich Bullinger (1504–1575) was the leader of the Reformed church of Zurich for forty-four years, from 1531 to 1575. During his lifetime he published 119 works in Latin and German, many of which were translated into other languages, including especially English and Dutch. His works found their way to nearly every corner of Europe as well as to the British colonies in America. Bullinger's extant correspondence numbers twelve thousand pieces. He was responsible to a large extent for the First Helvetic Confession (1536). He was the author of the Second Helvetic Confession (1566), which became the most authoritative of all the Reformed confessions in the sixteenth century. The great influence of Bullinger on the formation and development of the Reformed tradition can, therefore, hardly be denied. But his stature within that tradition has been largely obscured by John Calvin and by the followers of Calvin. Indeed, it has become usual for historians as well as the general public to give the name Calvinism to the entire Reformed tradition, thus using a sector of it to characterize the whole and eliminating central parts of Reformed thought, in particular, the federal stream. No account of the Reformed movement is complete that does not include Bullinger and federalism. In recent decades, this historical distortion of the Reformed tradition has begun to be overcome, and Bullinger's thought has begun to emerge from obscurity.[7]

Bullinger became the chief pastor of the Reformed church at Zurich on December 13, 1531, just two months after the disastrous defeat of the Zurich forces at Kappel. Huldrych

Zwingli, who had led the Reformation in Zurich, died in that battle. Bullinger, then twenty-seven years old, had served as a teacher in the Cistercian Monastery at Kappel from 1523 to 1529; he was, in fact, instrumental in bringing the monastery to a Reformed position in 1525. From 1529 until the victory of the Roman Catholic forces at Kappel in October 1531, Bullinger was pastor of the church at Bremgarten, where his father had been chaplain and dean for many years. But according to the Second Peace of Kappel, Bullinger was exiled from Bremgarten, and in late November he went to Zurich. Within three weeks of his arrival, he had accepted the city council's invitation to replace the fallen Zwingli as leader of the Zurich church.[8]

The One and Eternal Testament or Covenant of God: Historical Context

The four years following the defeat at Kappel was a period of some confusion and turmoil for the Reformed church at Zurich and elsewhere in the Swiss Confederation. Bullinger was at the center of events as they unfolded.

Only three months after he became the spiritual leader of Zurich he faced a daunting challenge from Leo Jud, a leading minister who had worked shoulder to shoulder with Zwingli from the earliest years of the Reformation. Jud felt that the established system of Christian discipline, which was under the authority of the magistracy, had proven a failure. Jud wanted to replace that system with an ecclesiastical morals court, independent of the government, with the power of excommunication. It took Bullinger until December 1533 to convince Jud of the perils of his proposal and to bring him back to support of the existing system. Bullinger believed that Jud's proposal to take moral discipline out of the hands of the magistrates smacked of Anabaptism, and this suspicion was strengthened when it became clear that Jud had come under the spell of Caspar Schwenckfeld. Not only did Schwenckfeld deny that the church was subject to the magistracy but he also rejected the authority of the Old Testament and argued against infant baptism. These teachings were held by the Anabaptists, who were quite active during this period in the Reformed areas of the Swiss Confederation and who seemed to be meeting with some success, especially in the Bernese territories.

A disputation between the Reformed and the Anabaptists was held at Zofingen in July 1532. Three of the topics for debate—the definition of the church, of Christian discipline, and of the magistracy—weighed heavily on Bullinger's mind during that summer. He had already published a book in 1531 opposing the Anabaptists and was highly regarded as an expert on them. Prior to the Zofingen disputation, Berchtold Haller of Bern had consulted Bullinger on how to deal with the Anabaptists on the matter of the authority of the Old Testament. After the disputation, Haller and Bullinger corresponded on the topic of proper punishment for Anabaptists, especially whether they should be subject to the death penalty. Bullinger expressed the opinion that they should be. Later, in the shadow of the Anabaptist revolution in Münster and the bloody nature of the Anabaptist regime there, Bullinger advised the Zurich city council in 1535 that recalcitrant Anabaptists ought to be executed.[9]

It was within the context of this continuing debate about church, state, and Christian discipline that Bullinger wrote *The One and Eternal Testament or Covenant of God*, apparently in October and November 1533. Early in October he had traveled to Constance to visit his friend Ambrosius Blarer. Their conversations must have included discussions about Jud, Schwenckfeld, the Anabaptists, and the specific issues involved. Shortly after Bullinger's return to Zurich, Blarer wrote to him, imploring that Bullinger send "what you recently promised to send concerning the single testament or one covenant." Blarer later reported that he had received the manuscript in early December.[10] Bullinger subsequently wrote to another friend, Joachim Vadian, that he had written *The Covenant* "against the many heresies rising up today."[11]

There is, then, no doubt that *The Covenant* was written in the midst of and as a response to controversy. It was not the case, however, that Bullinger came up with the idea of the covenant only to meet the exigencies of the immediate context. Rather, he had developed the covenant concept and applied it in a variety of situations for nine years prior to the publication of *The Covenant* in 1534. Beginning in 1525, he employed a fairly well developed concept of the covenant in several manuscripts,[12] in letters,[13] and in several publications, most notably in his work against the Anabaptists.[14]

It should also not be supposed that Bullinger utilized the covenant only in the midst of controversy with the radicals. After publishing *The Covenant*, he made the covenant the central motif of his theology. The covenant became a prominent feature in his commentaries; in fact, *The Covenant* was appended to his commentary on the epistles of Paul and the other apostles, which he published in 1537. Further, the covenant was the major organizing principle in many of the works that Bullinger published between 1534 and 1575; in other works it is just below the surface or constitutes an important sub-theme. The covenant was, in short, at the center of Bullinger's thought.[15]

The One and Eternal Testament or Covenant of God: The Argument

In this treatise which provided the most important source of federalism, Bullinger viewed the covenant as the divine frame-work for human life, both religious and civil, from the beginning of the world until the last judgment. The opening section of the work discussed the meanings of the word *testamentum*—a last will, a promise, or a covenant—and Bullinger assured the reader that he was using the term in the third sense, as covenant. He then dealt in the second part with the covenant as it was made with Abraham and concluded that the seed, or posterity, of Abraham was all of those faithful to God and their children. The third section had to do with the conditions of the covenant. God had promised that he would be all-sufficient. The conditions for humans were "to walk before God and be upright" (Gen. 17:1), that is, to have faith in God and love for the neighbor.

Bullinger affirmed that Scripture in its entirety taught the covenant and its conditions. The moral law was a restatement of these conditions, and the magistrate had been designated to enforce the conditions of the covenant among God's people. The prophets taught the same covenant. Christ renewed and confirmed the covenant. And the apostles after Christ taught the same covenant that had been made with Abraham. There was, in short, only one covenant of God. The ceremonial law had been given to the Jews as a support for the covenant, to help keep them true to the covenant; but the ceremonies had nothing to do with the essence of the covenant except that they were typological foreshadowings of Jesus Christ.

When Christ fulfilled the promise of the covenant it had been necessary to change the sacraments of the covenant. The old sacraments—circumcision and the Passover—had been fulfilled by Christ. They were replaced, therefore, by Baptism and the Eucharist. Just as infants before Christ had been initiated into the covenant and the church of God by circumcision, so they were, after Christ, enrolled among the people of God by baptism. Bullinger concluded the treatise with a section in which he argued that Christianity had begun with Adam when the covenant had first been made with humans. It was, there-fore, the oldest religion of all.

Of all the published works of Bullinger *The Covenant* was the most important and influential. It was the seminal work of the federal tradition in Western thought and marks Bullinger as the initiator of this tradition in a very specific sense. This work quietly began a movement that made federal thought a hallmark of the Reformed tradition both on the Continent and in England and Scotland by the end of the sixteenth century. During this period, federal theology and political philosophy were emerging out of the heritage shaped by Bullinger and were evolving into the forms that permeate modern democratic societies. It was, for example, this federal tradition, with explicit theological, ethical, and political dimensions, that was taken to the new world by the Puritans and used as the model for the colonies of New England. Bullinger's *The Covenant* was the fountainhead of federalism within the Reformed tradition and beyond. As Emanuel Graf von Korff wrote many years ago, Bullinger was "the first true federal theologian."[16]

The Use of the Covenant Idea by Other Early Reformed Leaders

It is true that others used the covenant idiom during the 1520s and early 1530s, prior to the publication of *The Covenant,* but none of them can be called a federal theologian in the way that Bullinger can be so designated after the publication of this treatise.

Zwingli is a case in point. Zwingli and Bullinger developed an idea of covenant at about the same time, during the period from 1525 to 1527. Most probably they collaborated with each other on the topic. There was ample opportunity for such collaboration. Bullinger was in Zurich for each of the three disputations with the Anabaptists in 1525, and he spent five months there in 1527. Zwingli's concept of the covenant was similar to Bullinger's in this period. Zwingli taught that there was only one covenant, one people of God, and one church in history. Though he hinted at the bilateral nature of the covenant, he did not strongly and clearly affirm the mutual responsibilities of God and humans. Nor did he make the covenant the center of his theology; for Zwingli, the covenant motif remained essentially a basis for his reply to the Anabaptist teachings on baptism.[17]

Johannes Oecolampadius of Basel (d. 1531) also made use of the covenant idea. He was, in fact, the only contemporary author whom Bullinger cited in *The Covenant* in support of his own view that there was only one covenant in history. But

Bullinger chose his quotation from Oecolampadius carefully, even deleting material in order to tailor the Baseler's viewpoint to his own. Oecolampadius posited an old and a new covenant; he had a two-covenant scheme that gave his concept a very different slant from Bullinger's. Nowhere did Oecolampadius state clearly the bilateral nature of the covenant. His idea of covenant was therefore incomplete and really quite different from Bullinger's.[18]

Martin Bucer (or Butzer), (1491–1551) was the third leader of the Reformed movement who can be viewed as an early covenant thinker. He seems to have arrived at the idea of the covenant in 1527 in his commentary on the Gospels, where he affirmed that there is only one covenant in history and declared that faith and love were stipulations of the covenant. This was after Zwingli's idea of the covenant had appeared in print in his writings against the Anabaptists. Bucer, however, no more than Zwingli, made the covenant the center of his theology.[19] Therefore, of those who used the covenant idiom prior to 1534, only Zwingli and Bucer formulated the term in a way close to its usage by Bullinger, but neither of them can be called a federal theologian in the sense in which the name applies to Bullinger.

The Development of Swiss Covenant Thought in the Mid-Sixteenth Century

The influence of Bullinger as the first federal theologian was immense. Of those whom he influenced in Switzerland during his own lifetime, the most important was Wolfgang Musculus (1497–1563) of Bern. Musculus posited two covenants. God made the first general covenant with Noah after the flood (Gen. 8:21; 9:9–11); it was a temporal covenant demonstrating the general grace of God. The second, special and eternal, covenant was first made explicitly with Abraham, although all the faithful from the time of Adam had participated in it. God promised to be the God of all those who were in this covenant. The conditions for humans were faith and obedience. Like Bullinger, Musculus also distinguished the essential things of the covenant, God's promise and the human conditions, from the appendages to the covenant, such as the promise of the land of Canaan. In the end, for Musculus as for Bullinger, there was one covenant, one people of God, and one church from Adam to the end of the world.[20]

Several scholars have attempted to show that John Calvin (1509–1564) was a covenant theologian and that he was the source of much of the later federal theology.[21] Calvin certainly made use of the covenant idiom. Indeed, at times, he sounds much like Bullinger in his affirmation of the unity of the covenant. But Calvin, like Oecolampadius, distinguished between two covenants or testaments: he spoke of the spiritual covenant, or the new testament, which was equivalent to the gospel; and he referred to the carnal covenant, or the old testament, by which he meant the law. The new testament, or the gospel, had existed since Adam. Though it had been only a feeble spark in Adam's day, the spiritual covenant had become clearer and clearer through the centuries, until it was fully revealed in Christ. But this was hardly a new idea in the sixteenth century. In fact, Calvin's idea of "covenant" was hardly different from Augustine's notion of the unity of faith in the Old and New Testaments.

Augustine had also affirmed the unity of faith and had asserted that there was only one church in history from Adam until the end of the world. His purpose was to establish the Old Testament as Christian Scripture and to defend Catholic baptism against the Donatists. He made the same distinction as Calvin between the carnal old covenant and the spiritual new testament or covenant. Bullinger quoted Augustine at length in *The Covenant* to support his affirmation of the unity of the people of God. But Augustine did not think in terms of a bilateral covenant; he was not a covenant theologian. Nor was Calvin a covenant theologian, despite the fact that he often referred to the covenant and spent many, many pages in his *Institutes* writing about the covenant.[22]

The Reformed Tradition: Federalism and Calvinism

As theological teaching developed in the era of the Reformation, three distinctive ways emerged to express the Protestant doctrine of salvation by grace (*sola fide* and *sola gratia*). The first was Luther's distinction between law and gospel, along with his emphasis on the bondage of the will and passive righteousness. The second was Calvin's doctrine of double predestination and election, which carefully protected both *sola fide* and *sola gratia* and tended to preclude any concept of a conditional or bilateral covenant. The third way was Bullinger's federal pattern, with the notion of a bilateral covenant as the vehicle through which God worked with the human race in history. An emphasis on one of these three ways did not necessarily exclude elements of the others. Luther, for example, also taught the election of the saints, and he had an idea of testament or covenant in the Augustinian sense. Nor did Calvin's doctrine of double predestination prevent him from dealing with law and gospel or with testament or covenant, again in the Augustinian sense.

Bullinger disagreed with Luther on law and gospel: he did not agree that the law had been abolished by Christ. He did, however, believe with Luther in the election of the saints, though he could not accept Calvin's doctrine of double predestination. But Bullinger was the only one of the three who can correctly be called a covenant or federal theologian. His entire theological system was organized around the idea of a bilateral, conditional covenant, made first by God with Adam, a covenant that would endure until the end of the world.

The differences between Bullinger and Calvin formed the basis for the two alternative, though related, strands within the Reformed tradition—Federalism and Calvinism. It has become usual among historians to reduce Reformed thought in the sixteenth and seventeenth centuries to Calvinism. This reductionism has even led many to refer to the Westminster Confession as a Calvinist theological statement. It is a Reformed confession, but it is most certainly much more a product of the federal tradition than of the Calvinist element.[23]

Bullinger and the Development of the Theological Tradition of Federalism

As the federal theology developed in the sixteenth and seventeenth centuries, it added terminology and concepts that went beyond Bullinger's original statement of federalism in *The Covenant*. David Alexander Weir, in his work on the origins of federal theology in the sixteenth century, provides a summary of the emphases that emerged later in the federal tradition. They posited two covenants, Weir observes, a covenant of works and a covenant of grace. The covenant of works was made with Adam and Eve, and thus with the entire human race, prior to the fall into sin. This covenant was conditional and mutual: the human conditions were not to eat of the fruit of the tree of the knowledge of good and evil, to keep the Sabbath, and to keep the commandments of God that were written upon their hearts; the divine condition was the promise to bless humans if they kept God's commandments. The covenant of grace, on the other hand, was unconditional. Humans were unable to keep the covenant of works. But God acted in Christ to uphold the divine promise. Christ fulfilled the demands of the covenant of works and extended the benefits of obedience to the elect, who were saved by grace alone through the covenant of grace. The covenant of works bound all humans; the covenant of grace had to do only with believers, with those called to faith, with the elect. Finally, Weir notes, the covenant had a prelapsarian sacrament, the tree of life.[24]

Many of these later emphases can be found in Bullinger's thought, at least in embryo, if not in *The Covenant,* then in other works. Bullinger did not think in terms of two covenants, but he did affirm that the covenant was first made with Adam and Eve. Nor did he speak specifically of a covenant before the fall. However, he did state, in *The old fayth* (ET 1541), that God had given a law to Adam and Eve in Paradise, prior to the fall. This law was expressed in the commandment not to eat of the tree of the knowledge of good and evil, or, to put it more succinctly, that they must love and obey God.[25] Even though he did not refer here to a covenant prior to the fall, it is implied in saying that love and obedience were the conditions applicable to Adam and Eve in creation. Bullinger then went on to state that after the fall God transferred the curse from humans to Christ in "the first promise and the authentic gospel" (Gen. 3:15).[26] With that promise, God made the eternal covenant with Adam for the restitution of the human race.[27] Many elements of the later formulations, therefore, were present or implicit in Bullinger's thought as early as 1537.

Bullinger's thought, however, did not require two covenants. The two covenant concept became a necessity because of the two trends within Calvinist Reformed thought in the later sixteenth century. First, there was the rational logical thrust, often referred to as the new Protestant scholasticism; and second, there was the high Calvinist idea of double predestination.

Both of these trends were foreign to Bullinger's thought. He held to a doctrine of single predestination. His approach may seem at times to verge on universalism, but he always took care to guard God's free grace. He dealt with election within the context of the covenant that God had made with the entire human race. Having accepted the covenant sign of baptism, humans obligated themselves to fulfill the covenant conditions of faith and love. If they met the conditions, they belonged to the elect. Bullinger stayed carefully on this practical, historical level; he was content to leave unresolved the inherent tension between his understanding of the biblical teachings of a single predestination and the universal atonement within the context of the covenant. Bullinger did not so much as mention predestination in *The Covenant.*[28]

By the 1580s and 1590s the high Calvinist ideal of double predestination was becoming commonplace within the Calvinist branch of the Reformed tradition. It was especially the rational-

ists who embraced this approach to predestination. The development of the doctrine of the two covenants was closely
connected with their understanding of the eternal decree. The
covenant of works was conditional. The entire human race was
obligated to fulfill the condition of keeping God's law. None, of
course, was able to fulfill this condition; the law was unfulfill-
able. The covenant of grace applied only to God's elect. It was
unconditional; under its provisions the elect were saved purely
by God's grace. God's decree of election and reprobation was
thus executed within the framework of the two covenants. The
federal perspective gave historical, biblical, and existential
moorings to the double predestination scheme. Franciscus
Gomarus and William Perkins are good examples of this type of
federal theology.[29]

While the federal perspective tended to blunt the rational,
logical thrust of high Calvinism, some seventeenth-century
federal theologians felt uncomfortable with the idea that the
covenant of grace was totally unconditional. They returned to
Bullinger's earlier perspective and restored the conditional
element in the covenant of grace. Among them were Johannes
Cocceius[30] and Moïse Amyraut[31] as well as the federal theologians in England and New England who developed the idea of
"preparation."[32]

Though the federal stream of Reformed thought develops
beyond its explicit formation in Bullinger, the basic shape of
federalism is stated or implied in his work. In this way, *The
Covenant* is clearly the fountainhead of theological federalism.

Bullinger and the Development of Political Federalism

The political tradition of federalism also finds its roots in
Bullinger's thought. In *The Covenant* he included a section in
which he discussed "civil or judicial laws" in connection with the
covenant condition of love. God's people needed the magistrate
and his laws to govern every aspect of life. In other writings he
was even more specific on the role of the magistrate. The
Christian magistrate was sovereign in Christian societies, and it
was his duty to enforce the conditions of the covenant. The first
condition, love of God, encompassed religious life; and the
second, love of the neighbor, covered all civil relationships.
Like the Old Testament priests, pastors in Reformed communities taught God's will to the people and to the magistrate. The
civil ruler, like the rulers in the Old Testament, enforced God's
will in society. The role of the civil government included also
the care of religion and the church. The covenant was, there-

fore, the centerpiece of the Christian religion and the cornerstone of the Christian state. It was the moral foundation of society and of religion.[33]

Though Bullinger's political system does not contain all the elements of later federalism, he nevertheless sets forth the frame of a federal order.

For example, Bullinger provides checks on civil rulers. In later political federalism, society was understood as based on a covenant or a contract, implicit or explicit, among the participants, and sovereignty was vested in the people as a covenanted community. Human nature was viewed ambiguously, that is, as having potential for both good and evil. The federal tradition developed notions of the limitations of power in both church and state and of governmental checks and balances.

The first fairly well developed theory of such federal relationships appeared in *A Defense of Liberty Against Tyrants,* published in 1579 and almost certainly written by Philippe Duplessis-Mornay.[34] Mornay's justification of resistance to tyranny rested upon his understanding of society as a series of covenants, religious and political, which made the civil rulers responsible both to God and to the people, who were the locus of civil sovereignty. Mornay's view of the religious covenant was nearly identical to Bullinger's. His concept of the political covenant was also similar to Bullinger's in terms of the manner in which the ruler was obligated to uphold God's law and to enforce the conditions of the covenant, but he went beyond Bullinger in asserting that the ruler could be deposed if he did not keep his covenant with God and the people.

The first systematic, fully developed articulation of federal political philosophy came from Johannes Althusius in his *Politics,* published in 1603.[35] In this work, he referred frequently to Mornay.

Other expressions of federal political thought and social covenant/contract theory were developed by such thinkers as John Winthrop, Samuel Rutherford, Thomas Hobbes, and John Locke. Federal political thought spread rapidly during the seventeenth and eighteenth centuries. It was brought to America by early settlers in the British colonies—the Anglicans in Virginia, the Puritans of New England in particular, and later the Presbyterians in the Middle Colonies. It gathered strength during the colonial period and acquired the characteristics that identify a distinctively American federal tradition. It was taught in the colonial colleges. The most striking example occurred in the teaching of John Witherspoon, a Scottish federal theologian and political philosopher at the

College of New Jersey, who taught James Madison. The federal tradition of the colonies influenced the formation of colonial charters and, later, state constitutions. Federalism was the social and political air breathed by the leaders of the American Revolution and by Madison and his colleagues at the Constitutional Convention. From them, federalism formed the basis of the Articles of Confederation and the Constitution of the United States of America.

As with theological federalism, political federalism develops beyond Bullinger's views. But later expansions only demonstrate that he is a primary source of the movement.

2

The Development of the Federal
Theological Tradition

From the era of Bullinger onward, the stream of theology with the covenant at its core flourished. Because the word "federal," as pointed out earlier, derives from the Latin *foedus*, which means covenant, this movement has been appropriately named federal theology. In a very real sense, federalism flowed down the Rhine from Zurich and, over the course of the sixteenth and seventeenth centuries, became a major sector of theology within the Reformed churches of Switzerland, Germany, the Netherlands, Britain, and eventually New England. Reformed faith of a federal type was, for example, a pervasive force in the religious-political movement in the Lowlands that threw off the oppressive rule of Spain and, in 1579, established the United Provinces, a confederation of Dutch provinces. Centers of federal theology emerged also in Germany, especially Heidelberg, Herborn, and Bremen.

The influence of Bullinger is abundantly clear in the continental development of federalism as well as in the Reformed churches of Scotland and England and, through them, in the British colonies of North America. His theological and political formulation of covenant thought, for example, can be discerned in the movement that produced the National Covenant in Scotland in 1638 and the Solemn League and Covenant between Reformed movements in England and Scotland in 1643. This alliance led to the calling of the Westminster Assembly and the formulation of the Westminster Confession. In league with the Independents under Cromwell, this movement overthrew Charles I. Though events did not lead in the direction planned by the Scottish-English coalition of Reformed federalists, the character of British society was changed decisively by the revolution they began.

In New England, federalism so permeated the social patterns—in civil government, in the churches, and in commerce—that it is difficult to find more than variations of this
perspective there. Federal thought flowed into the life of the
other British colonies in America, developed a distinctive tradition, and gave shape to the society that became the United
States of America.

The influence of Bullinger was mediated in part through
Reformed leaders who came to Zurich to study with him and with
his colleague Peter Martyr Vermigli. For example, many Reformed leaders, such as Zacharias Ursinus and Kaspar Olevianus, spent time there as students. Olevianus, in particular,
expressed his indebtedness to Bullinger. Even more, Bullinger's
federal views were spread through his writing. The Latin version
of *The Covenant* was circulated widely in Reformed areas, as was
the German translation that Bullinger issued in the same year.
His work in basic theology, with the covenantal perspective at its
center, was published as *Der alt gloub* in 1537 and was among the
first of his works to appear in English, published in 1541 as *The
old fayth*. At least as important also were his sermons, issued at
different times and known in English under the title *Decades*
because the sermons were collected there in groups of ten. The
Decades were published in Latin in 1552. In 1558 these sermons
appeared in a German translation known as the *Hausbuch* and
was circulated widely in the German-speaking sectors of the
Reformed communities from Switzerland, through Germany,
and into the Lowlands. It went through four German editions
prior to 1600. A Dutch version was published in 1563 and, with
the full or partial text, had gone through thirteen editions by
1622. At least one sermon from the *Decades* was available in
English as early as 1549. Excerpts from the entire work were
translated into English and published in 1566. The first complete
edition appeared in England in 1577 and was reprinted in 1584
and 1587. In the 1570s and 1580s it became a standard text for
instructing clergy and students of theology. The *Decades* appeared in French in 1559–1560 and had gone through three
editions by 1565. Bullinger's larger systematic treatise in theology, *Summa Christenlicher Religion* (1556), was, like his other works,
circulated in all Reformed communities and was published in
English as *Commonplaces of the Christian Religion* in 1572.[1]

The Early Spread of Federalism in the Lowlands

One of the areas where the influence of Bullinger's federalism had an early and important impact was among the Dutch.

In the Netherlands his influence derived in particular from the direct and indirect acquaintance of preachers and laity with such works of Bullinger's as *The Covenant* and the *Decades* and from their use in the preaching and writing of Reformed leaders in the Lowlands.

Johannes Anastasius Veluanus was an early leader of the Reformation in the Netherlands who demonstrated the influence of Bullinger's covenantal theology. Though little is known of his early life, he was by 1544 a Roman Catholic chaplain in the armed forces. Around 1550 he converted to the Reformed faith and, except for "one shameful recantation," to use his own description, remained true to the recovered biblical faith of the Reformation for the rest of his life. In 1554 he published a *Guide for Laity to Christian Faith*,[2] a work that took covenant thought into the homes and lives of ordinary people of Reformed persuasion in the Lowlands.[3]

As the federal thought of Veluanus appears in the *Guide*, the covenant was first made with Adam. Subsequently it was renewed with Abraham and with his successors in faith throughout the Old Testament. In Christ the covenant was confirmed and fulfilled. Indeed, from the beginning, God's covenant with humanity was based on the promise of Christ. Faith is the central condition of the covenant; a secondary condition is living a virtuous life. Neither condition can be fulfilled by humans alone but can be met only with God's help through Christ and the Holy Spirit. "God makes a covenant with the Christian," he wrote, "and the Christian makes a covenant with God. Baptism is a true sign of both, just as circumcision was a covenant sign between God and Abraham's children (Gen. 17:11–14; Rom. 4:11)."[4]

Gellius Snecanus (1520–?) was another leader of the Reformed movement among the Dutch illustrating the influence of Bullinger and federalism. In his primary work, *A Methodical Description of God's Covenant of Grace*,[5] published in 1584, he followed Bullinger in affirming that the covenant or testament of God was a covenant of grace. Made first with Adam, and renewed with Abraham, it was confirmed through Jesus Christ as the mediator and guarantor of the covenant. As such, it was the instrument through which God adopted Adam and the seed of Abraham and made them heirs through the fulfillment of the covenant in Christ. By grace through the covenant, God liberated humans from bondage to works and to the freedom of faith. Throughout its three economies—before the law, under the law, and after the law—this covenant of grace retained its unity so that it included both the Old Testament and the New. The covenant, also in the form of a testament, was sealed through the death of Christ. In him, by faith, the sins of humanity were forgiven and the covenant revealed as eternal. Of the covenant with Abraham, he wrote: "In these few words is included whatever pertains to true faith and love, both towards God and towards humanity. The sum of the entire Scripture and of piety consists in these two conditions of the divine covenant."[6] In agreement also with Bullinger, Snecanus saw the sacraments of the covenant as the signs and seals of the covenant in both Old and New Testament. The children of faithful covenant members were included in the covenant through baptism. Only those who fulfilled the conditions of faith and love, however, could ultimately be regarded as holding membership on their own in the covenant.[7]

Cornelius Wiggertz (ca. 1550–1624) was another Dutch leader influenced by the federalism of Bullinger. Known as "the great firebrand of the Dutch church,"[8] Wiggertz was explicitly an exponent of universalism and was an early casualty of the reaction to what became known later as Arminianism. He was defrocked and excommunicated in 1598. Among the persons who signed the decree was Franciscus Gomarus (1563–1641), a professor of theology at the University of Leiden, the great opponent of Jacobus Arminius (1560–1609), a professor of theology at Leiden[9] who gave his name to the Arminian movement.

Wiggertz took Bullinger's view of the covenant to a position of explicit universalism that was not present in Bullinger himself. In the same way, many high Calvinists in the late sixteenth century took Calvin's view of predestination to a level that cannot be found explicitly in Calvin and encased it in an increasingly rigid rationalism.

Many of these high Calvinist thinkers were attracted to covenant thought. The federal idea, with its double aspect of works and grace, enabled them to shift the conditional element in the God-human relationship to the covenant of works, as it was eventually named, while making the covenant of grace unconditional. The two covenants thus became the vehicle by which God worked out the Eternal Decree of election and reprobation in history.

Early English Covenantal Thought

In Britain, focus on the covenant in theology appeared at least as early as *William Tyndale* (1492?–1536). Tyndale, a leader of the group in England, was attracted very early to the Protestant movement in Germany led by Martin Luther. Tyndale's special concern was to have the New Testament published in English, which at that time was forbidden. He therefore went to the Continent, visited Luther, and published the New Testament in 1526 in his own superb translation. Though not fully federal in his thought, Tyndale was moving in ways parallel to Bullinger in Switzerland. In the preface to the 1534 edition of his New Testament, Tyndale set forth the covenant as the theme of the whole of Scripture. This covenant of God, for Tyndale, was conditional. God had promised to give all of the "mercies and grace that Christ hath purchased for us," but this promise was made "upon the condition that we keep the lawe." Keeping the law meant two things: "The fyrst is a stedfast fayth and trust in Almightie God. . . . And the other is that we forsake evell and turne to God."[10] These conditions, faith and piety, were the same as Bullinger's, and there does seem to have been some influence on Tyndale from Zurich.[11]

Born in Yorkshire and educated at Cambridge, *Miles Coverdale* (1488?–1569) became a bishop of Exeter in the Anglican Church. He was a friend of William Tyndale's and, like Tyndale, gave attention to the place of the covenant in biblical Christian faith. With authorization from Henry VIII, Coverdale published the first English translation of the entire Bible, using all of Tyndale's rendition of the New Testament and as much of the Old Testament as Tyndale had done.

Though the influence of Bullinger on Tyndale seems definite but the relationships not established, the impact of Zurich on Coverdale is much clearer. Coverdale's first edition of the Bible was not authorized and was printed on the Continent, possibly in Zurich by Froschauer, the same printer that issued Bullinger's *The Covenant*. In his preface to his edition of the Bible, Coverdale took over much of the covenant theology found in Tyndale, which bore a strong resemblance to that of Bullinger. An even more specific link, however, was Coverdale's translation and publication of Bullinger's *Der alt gloub*, which appeared in English as *The old fayth* in 1541. Here is clear evidence of the direct influence of Bullinger on Coverdale. It also demonstrates beyond doubt the early influence of Bullinger on the rise of Puritan federal theology in Britain.[12]

A third English thinker influenced by Bullinger's covenant theology was *John Hooper* (?–1555), an Anglican bishop who was martyred by being burned at the stake during the Roman Catholic regime of Mary Tudor, as were Bishops Cranmer, Ridley, and Latimer. Already interested in the thought of Zwingli and Bullinger and apparently because of his acceptance of Zurich teachings, Hooper was compelled to leave England.

He went first to Strassburg in 1547 and then on to Zurich, where he spent two years, during which he began a personal friendship with Bullinger and became an even closer follower of Bullinger's thought. In a *Declaration of the Ten Holy Commandments*, which Hooper wrote and published in 1548 while in Zurich, he explains the covenant as an agreement between God and the human race, through which God obligated himself to aid and preserve humans and to give them eternal life, while humans were bound in the covenant to obey God and to love God. The Ten Commandments, in Hooper's view, expressed the conditions binding humans in the covenant.[13]

In addition to their focus on the covenant as central to Christian faith, these early leaders of Protestantism in England also shared a moderate understanding of single predestination. The idea of a conditional covenant, which they espoused, contained an implicit universalism that was modified by their teaching on predestination and election. They were therefore in general agreement with Bullinger on this issue. The Zurich version of covenant thought was, however, changed as Calvin's ideas on predestination began to filter into England after the middle of the century. When the next covenant thinkers appeared on the scene, from the 1580s onward, their position had been influenced by the rationalism of the high Calvinist view, with its teaching of double predestination, that had been emerging in the latter part of the sixteenth century. As we shall see when we turn to the theology of Thomas Cartwright, Dudley Fenner, and William Perkins, federalism had an important function in that time as a means for avoiding both the stark, impersonal necessity of Calvinist logic and the perils of heterodoxy in theology.

The Emergence of the Double Covenant in German Federal Theology

At the same time that the influence of Bullinger's federalism was having its impact in the Netherlands and in Britain, his views were also spreading in Germany. In particular, important developments in federal theology were occurring there that became hallmarks of the movement in the seventeenth century. We shall look briefly at two of the central figures in this unfolding of the covenant concept in German theology— Ursinus in Heidelberg; and Olevianus, who taught first in Heidelberg and then became the founding rector of the Academy of Herborn, a university that served as a focal point of federal thought from its founding in 1584 onward.

Representing the second generation of Reformation scholarship, that is, one of those leaders who grew up in a Protestant context and studied with the first generation of Reformers, *Zacharias Ursinus* (1534–1583) was born in Breslau of a family with sufficient means to ensure an excellent education for him. Of a somewhat retiring and timid nature, the young Ursinus demonstrated himself to be a brilliant student. He studied in Wittenberg with Philip Melanchthon for seven years, from 1550 to 1557, becoming a convinced "Philippist" in theology and, in addition, acquiring a deep personal loyalty to Melanchthon. It was this background which apparently provided Ursinus with a bridge for his shift from Lutheran to Reformed faith. This change took place through contacts that he made on travels in Reformed areas of Germany and Switzerland, especially during two extended periods of study that he spent in Zurich, 1557 to 1558 and 1560 to 1561. There he came under the direct influence of Bullinger and Peter Martyr Vermigli.

It was with the recommendation of his teachers in Zurich that Ursinus was called to a chair of dogmatics in Heidelberg. He took up his teaching duties there in 1561. Two years later, in 1563, he, perhaps with Olevianus, wrote the Heidelberg Catechism.[14] This statement of faith, prepared for instruction of church members, is a remarkably experiential and irenic expression of Reformed doctrine and rapidly became a widely accepted norm of faith in Reformed communities.

The federal shape of the theology of Ursinus is illustrated well in the first question of his own Major Catechism: "What can one hold as a firm basis in life and as consolation in death?" The reply was: "That I am created by God in His image and for life eternal; and though I am placed in misery through the will of Adam, God in immense and free mercy has received me into his covenant of grace."[15]

In his theology, Ursinus combined the thought of Melanchthon with that of Bullinger and developed a distinctive and innovative form of federalism. The covenant between God and human beings who have faith was, for Ursinus, the entire subject of Scripture. Following Bullinger, he understood the moral law to be included in God's command to Abraham to walk before God in righteousness, and he discovered the gospel in God's promise to bless all humanity through Abraham's seed.[16]

Of the covenant of grace, Ursinus wrote:

> The covenant that God made with humans through the Mediator is a promise and a mutual pact by which God obligates himself through and because of the Mediator to forgive sins in those who

believe and to give them eternal life; in return humans obligate themselves to receive this great gift by true faith and to show true obedience to God, that is, to live according to His will. This mutual pact is confirmed by the sacramental signs.[17]

Illustrating how federal thought typically combined theological and political motifs into a unified perspective, Ursinus understood the authority of God through the covenant as judicial. Humans became liable to punishment as a consequence of sin, that is, because of their violation of their obligation to obey the commandments of God given in the covenant. God's authority, the sin of humanity that makes all humans liable to punishment, and God's promise of salvation—all were conceived juristically through God's covenant with the human race.[18]

A new element that Ursinus added to the emerging federal tradition, building in part on his background with Melanchthon, was the notion of the *foedus naturae*, covenant of nature, before the fall into sin. The covenant, in this innovative view, was not initiated first with Abraham or even Noah but was originated with the creation of the world. As such, it was written upon the human heart and promised eternal life to humans on the condition that they persevere in the moral commandments of the covenant. Ursinus apparently was the first of the federal theologians to formulate explicitly the notion of a covenant of nature that God made with the human race in creation. The concept can be found in his Major Catechism, which he composed in 1561 or 1562, even prior to his collaboration with Olevianus on the Heidelberg Catechism. Question 10 of his Major Catechism was: "What does the divine Law teach?" The answer was: "That God made a covenant with humanity in creation."[19] Though Ursinus did not draw out the implications of this covenant of nature that came to characterize the federal theology as it developed after him, it seems clear that he was the first to name the covenant of nature and locate its origination before the fall.

Kaspar Olevianus (1536–1587) was also a professor of dogmatics at Heidelberg and for a time a colleague of Ursinus's. Born in Trier, where his father was a baker, guild master, and later city councillor and tax collector, Olevianus received his early education in Roman Catholic schools in Trier and, in 1550, went to Paris and studied at the Sorbonne. Then, as John Calvin had done before him, he studied law at Orléans and Bourges, receiving his doctorate in jurisprudence from the latter faculty of law in 1557.

While engaged in his law studies, Olevianus joined the burgeoning Protestant movement, and, as the result of almost losing his own life attempting to rescue a friend from drowning, he decided to devote his life to the service of God. From Bourges, therefore, he went to Switzerland, where he spent time in Zurich studying theology with Peter Martyr Vermigli and Heinrich Bullinger. He also visited Lausanne and became acquainted with Theodore Beza.

He returned to Trier and began teaching. Soon, however, he attempted to turn Trier to the Protestant faith. Though his efforts were successful with the populace, the movement was put down by armed forces led by the Roman Catholic archbishop. Olevianus was arrested and condemned to death. He was rescued only by the intervention of Elector Frederick III of the Palatinate, who invited him to teach in Heidelberg. Olevianus became an instructor in preaching at the Collegium Sapientiae in 1560 and, the following year, professor of dogmatics in the university. The same year, he received his doctorate in theology.

After the death of Frederick III in 1576, his place as elector was taken by Ludwig VI, a Lutheran, who deposed and expelled the Reformed teachers, including Olevianus. After seven years in Berleburg, teaching the sons of Count Ludwig von Wittgenstein, Olevianus was called, in 1584, by Count John the Elder of Nassau-Dillenburg to become pastor in Herborn and, shortly thereafter, to take the lead in founding the Academy of Herborn, where he then served as professor of dogmatics. Olevianus is buried in Pfarrkirche in Herborn.[20]

In his theology, Olevianus continued the development of federal thought. He built on the work of Bullinger and others before him and took federalism nearer to its fully articulated form. Writing to Bullinger, Olevianus said, "Indeed, if there is any sound wisdom in Reformed thought, we owe it in large measure to you and to the clear genius of the Swiss."[21]

Olevianus developed his federal theology in two of his treatises, his exposition of the Apostles' Creed, *Expositio symboli apostolici* (1576), and another on the content of the covenant of grace, *De substantia foederis gratuiti* (1585). In these works, he assumed the double covenant scheme and taught that there was a covenant of nature before the fall into sin that had clear legal commands as its conditions. In this covenant, humans in their created nature were provided with a clear understanding of right and wrong. Obedience to the covenant could be focused on following the command not to eat of the forbidden fruit. Adam and Eve violated this covenant because they believed the false promise of the serpent that they would not die but would rather become god in their independence and knowledge.

Because Adam and Eve were the federal heads of the human race, their disobedience brought condemnation on all humans under the legal terms of the covenant.

From the depth of divine mercy, however, God provided another course, one that carried out the legal demands of the covenant of nature yet showed forth the glory of God by carrying forward the covenant in a different way. God instituted the covenant of grace, in which salvation was accomplished, not through the efforts of humans alone, but through God acting in Christ. Christ fulfilled the demands of the covenant of nature and, through that fulfillment, God granted faith unto salvation to a certain number of fallen humans, that is, to the elect.

The covenant of nature, therefore, is conditional in that it depends upon the obedience of humanity to the divine commands, an obedience in which humanity fails and falls. The covenant of grace is unconditional, is completely dependent upon the will and action of God, yet fulfills in Christ the conditions of the covenant of nature. God in Christ became human, carried out the command of obedience, and offered salvation to the elect. While the first covenant rested upon grace and works, the second relied exclusively on God's grace. Here we see the origins of the way in which the double covenant scheme came to be fitted neatly with the double predestinarian pattern of the high Calvinist rationalists.

The importance and originality of Olevianus must be emphasized. While he drew on the federal tradition from Bullinger onward, Olevianus provided formulations and perspectives that take federalism to a distinctively new level of development. This can be seen in his elaboration of the double covenant and in his making more explicit and specific the juristic, political significance of federalism. So crucial was his place in the federal tradition that Heinrich Heppe regarded him as the "real founder of the developed federal theology."[22] And Ludwig Diestel said, "We perceive in Olevian the special foundation of the federal idea."[23]

These judgments can be understood when the federal theology of Olevianus is examined carefully. First, more than anyone before him, he not only utilized the covenant as the central concept of his thought but also deployed it more extensively as the principle by which to organize his entire theological system. Second, he extends the meaning of the double covenant idea. Whereas prior to him the notion of a covenant of nature had been used by Ursinus to mean a covenant of works with Adam before the fall, Olevianus understood this covenant of nature to be also a covenant *with* nature and with the entire created order. The covenant pervades the world as that which places the divine stamp of pattern, purpose, and grace on the whole of nature and history. Even further, Olevianus took the step of affirming that the divine nature itself must be understood by means of the covenant. There was a covenantal relation between the Father and the Son within the Trinity, in which the promise of the covenant and Christ as the sponsor/guarantor of the covenant were present in God prior to creation. Third, Olevianus enlarged the scope of the discussion about the covenant, so that attention was given not only to the origins of the covenant and its continuing presence as the pattern of history but also to the significance of the covenant for the life of the Christian believer. The covenant enters into the practical existence in faith with the assurance of salvation as well as having its source in Scripture and providing the basis of theological systematizing.

The education of Olevianus had prepared him to carry forward the combination of theological and political perspectives that became characteristic of the federal tradition in increasingly profound ways. The basis of this unified view had already been established by Bullinger, but Olevianus makes use of his juristic training to extend the social, political meaning of the covenant. For example, Adam was seen as representative human in the covenant of nature, a view with juristic provenance and political implications. In parallel fashion, Christ was the representative of the human race in the covenant of grace. Through the merit of Christ, the elect were relieved of the sentence of damnation that followed from disobeying the legal demands of the covenant of nature and offered salvation in the covenant of grace as heirs of Christ, whose death gave legal force to the covenant as testament. This development of federalism will bear fruit at Herborn as Althusius, absorbing these dimensions, articulated the first federal political philosophy.

The Maturing of the Federal Theology Among the British

As described earlier, the influence of Bullinger's thought appeared very early in Britain. The impact of federalism was important for the emergence of the Puritan movement in England and for the federal shape of thought within the Scottish churches, not only from Bullinger but also the extensions of the federal tradition in Heidelberg, Herborn, and elsewhere.

Dudley Fenner (1558?–1587) made important contributions

to the development of federalism among the Puritans. Though he died early, Fenner demonstrated himself to be a prolific and capable expositor of federal theology. In 1576, apparently while still in his teens, Fenner wrote *A Brief Treatise on the First Table of the Law*. Though this work did not yet exhibit the emerging characteristics of federalism, it made it clear that its young author had great promise as a theologian within the Reformed tradition. After he came under the direct influence of the federal theology, Fenner published *Sacra theologia* in 1585, a thoroughly federalist work showing him to be an exponent of the double covenant. Leonard Trinterud would attribute the origin of the double covenant idea to Fenner.[24] Though this does not appear to be so, Fenner apparently was the first to use the term "covenant of works."[25] In describing the covenant of works, Fenner stated that its condition was "perfect obedience." Then he specifically connected this covenant with "furthering and accomplishing the decree of predestination."[26] Further development of this connection between the double covenant scheme and the divine decree of predestination would come in the thought of William Perkins.

Fenner must be regarded as an important channel through whom the federal theology of Heidelberg, influenced strongly by Bullinger, flowed into Puritanism and the dissenter movements in England. But it was **William Perkins** (1558–1602) who, in *Armilla aurea,* or *A Golden Chaine* (1590), offered the most comprehensive treatment of federal theology for this period of Reformed thought in Britain. Of even greater importance, the high regard in which Perkins was held and the breadth of his influence among Puritans made it certain that federalism would become inextricably woven into the doctrine of the movement in England and in America.

In what by that time had become standard federalism and to some degree standard Reformed doctrine, Perkins taught that the covenant of God was twofold: a covenant of works and a covenant of grace. "God's covenant," he wrote, "is his contract with man, concerning the obtaining of life eternal, upon a certain condition."[27] In one sense, the covenant "consists of two parts: God's promise to man; and man's promise to God." In another sense, the covenant is twofold: of works and of grace. "The covenant of works," he continued, "is God's covenant made with the condition of perfect obedience, and is expressed in the moral law." The covenant of grace "is that whereby God freely promising Christ, and his benefits, exacts again of man, that he would by faith receive Christ, and repent of his sins."[28] This unconditional covenant of grace was revealed to Adam and Eve in Eden immediately after the fall into sin, unfolded through Abraham and his posterity, and was fulfilled in Jesus Christ.[29] In line with the federal views laid down by Bullinger, Perkins taught that the sacraments are "signs and pledges of God's mercy," and baptism is a "seal to confirm the believers' faith in the covenant of grace."[30] Infants "born of believing parents are holy before baptism, and baptism is but a seal of that holiness."[31]

Perkins made it clear in the preface that *A Golden Chaine* was a defense of the true doctrine of predestination against the new Pelagians, or the Arminians, in Holland. He abhorred their universalism, and, while arguing against their position, he affirmed a high Calvinist doctrine of double predestination. His use of the double covenant scheme is thus a particularly good example of how federalism blunted the rigidity of the double predestination system of the high Calvinist rationalists and gave it a more humane face.

In the wake of these developments on the Continent and in England, it is not surprising to find that federal thought began to appear in Scotland among the Reformed leaders there. One early and influential exponent of the federal theological perspective among the Scots was **Robert Rollock** (1555–1599).

After his preparation for ministry and ordination, Rollock became a pastor in Edinburgh and a leader of the Scottish church. In 1583, while still quite young, he became the first rector, or principal, of the University of Edinburgh, a position in which he remained until his death.

The work that best illustrated Rollock's federal views was *A Treatise of God's Effectual Calling*, written around 1594 and published in 1603. "The covenant of God generally," he wrote in this treatise, "is a promise under some one certain condition." Further, God's covenant "is twofold; the first is the covenant of works; the second is the covenant of grace." Of these, "the covenant of works, which may also be called a legal or natural covenant, is founded in nature, which by creation is pure and holy, and is the law of God, which in the first creation was engraven in man's heart." For Rollock, "the ground of the covenant of works was not Christ, nor the grace of God in Christ, but the nature of man in the first creation holy and perfect." From this it followed that the condition of the covenant of works was good works, and the condition of the covenant of grace was the grace of God in Jesus Christ, who fulfills the covenant of God, renders it operative in history through his death, and brings history and humanity to consummation in God.[32]

Graduated from the University of Glasgow in 1599, *John Cameron* (ca.1580–1625) was influenced by Rollock's federalism and pursued it further with studies in Heidelberg. He published his most important work on covenant thought at Heidelberg in 1608, where the federal legacy of Ursinus and Olevianus apparently continued after them.[33]

In 1618, Cameron was called to the Academy of Saumur in France, where he extended the influence of federalism within the Reformed communities of that country. Saumur had been founded by Philippe Duplessis-Mornay in the early years of the seventeenth century and became a center of federal thought and education for the Reformed churches of France.[34]

Cameron's federal theology, as it developed, was in part a reaction to the rigid rationalism of the high Calvinist teaching of double predestination that had emerged in the era prior to the Synod of Dort. This synod had issued its decrees in the very year that Cameron went to Saumur to teach. In his thought, Cameron reaffirmed the historical unfolding of the covenant and emphasized anew the conditional element in the covenant of grace, the condition of faith. He became widely known for his views, which some regarded as heretical, and made Saumur another center of federal thought.

Perhaps here is the appropriate place to mention *Moïse Amyraut* (1596–1664), a student of Cameron's at Saumur. He became a teacher there in 1626 and, like his mentor, emphasized history, experience, and revelation in his federal theology, rather than predestination. He refused to be drawn into the rationalism of the high Calvinists. Instead, he saw predestination as a human "*ex post facto* explanation of the work of God in salvation." The formulation by the high Calvinists of a rational system deduced from the doctrine of God's Eternal Decree of double predestination was, in Amyraut's view, damaging to the scriptural teaching both of the universal call of God to humanity and also of God's election of humanity in Christ.[35] Although Amyraut appealed to the writings of Calvin in support of his views on predestination and insisted that his teaching agreed with that of Calvin, he might have appealed to Bullinger as well.

The person who succeeded to Rollock's mantle of leadership in the Scottish Reformed movement was *Samuel Rutherford* (1600–1661), a federalist in his theological and political writing. The movement that carried on the work of earlier Scottish Reformers, of which Rutherford was a foremost leader, was called the Covenanters.

While minister in the Parish Kirk of Anwoth, beginning in

1627, Rutherford rose to prominence as a stern and rugged Covenanter. In 1636, during the time when Charles I of England was attempting to make the Scottish church Anglican, Rutherford was deposed from his ministerial office and forbidden to preach in any part of Scotland. The triumph of the Covenanters brought him out of exile in Aberdeen. He became the presiding cleric for the National Covenant, signed by an assembly meeting at Greyfriars Kirk in Edinburgh, in the spring of 1638. This covenant was reaffirmed at the Glasgow Assembly in November of the same year. In 1639 Rutherford was called to the chair of divinity at the University of St. Andrews. From that post he continued as part of the leadership that led to the Solemn League and Covenant of 1643, uniting the Scottish Covenanters and the English Puritans in a federal pact with powerful political, ecclesiastical, and military dimensions. This movement as it evolved led eventually to the overthrow of Charles I.

More than any other person, Rutherford provided an exposition of the theological and political principles undergirding and guiding the Reformed components of that movement. Rutherford did this in *Lex, Rex: the Law and the Prince,* published in 1644, and in *The Covenant of Life Opened; or, A Treatise of the Covenant of Grace,* published in 1655. These works provided the most comprehensive account of federalism in Britain up to that time. In them the close relation of religious faith and political action was made clear. Yet Rutherford also distinguished carefully and consistently between the appropriate functions of the church and those of the government. He showed throughout the influence upon him of the federal tradition from Bullinger onward.

Rutherford was both a product of and also a brilliant expositor of the federal context surrounding the Westminster Assembly and the Westminster Confession. The alliance between Reformed forces in Scotland and those in England eventually broke down. The Independent religious movement under Oliver Cromwell gained control, executed Charles I, and inaugurated the regime of Cromwell. Though England returned to the monarchy in 1660, in the restoration of Charles II to the throne, the era of Rutherford and Cromwell, with movements that came to power deeply imbued with federalism, reshaped the political life of Great Britain once and for all and gave a federal shape to the nation's future.

With the development of federal theology before us, we can now take a step backward in time and examine the development of federal political thought. Political federalism emerged alongside the theological movement. Indeed, in many federal thinkers, the theological and political are too closely intertwined to be separated and are difficult even to distinguish clearly. While political federalism did gradually take shape in ways that can be identified apart from theological federalism, the two elements are not separable until much later.

3

Federal Political Philosophy: Mornay and Althusius

Interwoven with the federal theology, political federalism was also emerging in the sixteenth and seventeenth centuries. Because of specialization and the separation of disciplines in twentieth-century universities, the relation between the theological and political elements in that earlier time is not always clear. Today, theology deals with religion, and political science with government and politics. The study of the covenant, consigned to theological studies, itself divided into separate disciplines, has generally been left to biblical scholars, who have dealt with it only as it appears in the Bible.[1] The notion of federalism has become the property of political science, history, and philosophy. All too often, as already noted, attention to federalism is limited to the era of the writing of the U.S. Constitution, and the history of the federal tradition is ignored. The wholeness of human experiencing is forgotten as fragments are parceled out to various academic specializations for isolated scrutiny. The sectors of human experience examined apart from their relation to one another become distorted and misunderstood. The close connection between covenant and social contract is overlooked. The significance of Thomas Hobbes's theology for his political philosophy is missed. And, strangest of all, the politics and ethics dominant in modern Western culture can be misread as "liberalism" without reference to the federal tradition.[2] A more accurate view of the past must be recovered in order that we can understand better who we are, where we are, and how best to plan for the future.

In works of political philosophy concerned with the post-Reformation period, an awareness that theological considerations have some relation to theories of government hovers around the edges. Yet scholars have not yet investigated what we call the "interweaving" in any satisfactory fashion. "Political science in Germany, Holland, Belgium, and other neighboring countries," wrote Robert Blakey in 1855, "was at this period greatly influenced by theological questions, both of doctrine and discipline."[3] He does not, however, explore what this influence was.

Discussions of *Vindiciae contra tyrannos* and of Johannes Althusius sometimes raise the issue of the theological context by which they were shaped, but careful discussion of the topic seldom takes place. Otto von Gierke, one of the great scholars on this era in general and on Althusius in particular, writes, "It was Althusius again who with creative genius embraced a system and grounded on a theoretical principle the federalistic ideas fermenting in the world of events and in the opinion of his own religious and political environment."[4] In another place he repeats this generalization in different words: "It was the work of Johannes Althusius to give logical unity to the federal ideas that simmered in the ecclesiastical and political circles in which he lived, and to construct an audacious system of thought in which they all found their place."[5]

George H. Sabine seems aware that some relationship exists. Because he deplores even the possibility that political thought might be based on theology or on the Bible, he fails to do more than suggest, mainly by denial, what the connection might be.[6] Ludwig Gumplowicz seems to assume that there is a general influence of Reformed thought on the development of federal politics without spelling out what this means.[7]

Quentin Skinner appears to regard theological and political federalism as totally unrelated. He refers to "the peculiarly Calvinist concept of the covenanting community"[8] with a discussion of Christopher Goodman and John Knox. He picks up the covenant theme again with a discussion of Mornay's use of the covenant. He states, "This contract (*pactum*) is wholly separate from the idea of the religious covenant (*foedus*) which the Huguenot theorists also invoke," "this contract" referring to a "purely political contract," which had its basis in scholasticism.[9] He goes on to speak of "the epoch-making move from a purely religious theory of resistance, depending on the idea of a covenant to uphold the laws of God, to a genuinely political theory of revolution, based on the idea of a contract" and of the "fully political theory of revolution, founded on a recognizably modern, secularized thesis about the natural rights and original sovereignty of the people," which he suggests leads to Locke's theory.[10] The most incomprehensible example of his dichotomized interpretation occurs when he refers to the secular nature of Althusius's political thought. After reading the literature, we must agree with Gottlob Schrenk, who provides a succinct understatement of the situation: "This influence of theological federalism on political theory has still to be investigated thoroughly."[11] In these chapters, we are making a beginning on this exploration.

The major figure in the development of an explicit federal political philosophy is Johannes Althusius. In order to suggest the theological and social background of his work in the Reformed communities of Europe, we shall look also at the *Vindiciae contra tyrannos*, or *A Defense of Liberty Against Tyrants*, a work that was published anonymously in 1579. It is more than coincidence that the *Vindiciae* was published in the same year that the Dutch, under William the Silent, united by their Reformed federal faith and having thrown off the tyrannical yoke of Roman Catholic Spain, established the United Provinces with its explicitly federal political form.

Mornay and the *Vindiciae*

Though the author of the *Vindiciae* used the pseudonym Junius Brutus at the time of publication, it has been established with a high degree of probability that the author was Philippe Duplessis-Mornay.[12] Mornay, in this work, was apparently the first among the federalists to use the covenant idea to justify resistance to tyrannical rulers. Mornay's work evoked immediate response for and against its views. Its critics were most obviously those who held to a view of the divine right of kings and regarded as radical any attempts to undermine the direct dependence upon God of the authority of monarchs. Those who tended to agree with Mornay were the groups seeking religious grounding for calling tyrannical kings to account before the divine bar of justice.

Mornay's treatise, however, was more than a justification for resistance, important as that aspect of the work turned out to be. It was also an argument for constitutionalism and the sovereignty of the people, also based on a covenantal perspective. It must be seen, therefore, as a contribution to the rise of federal political philosophy. Though Mornay's theological conception of the covenant bore striking resemblance to that of Bullinger, his political use of the federal principle varied significantly from Bullinger's and was much more radical and forward-looking than was the political use of the covenant by the more conservative leader of Zurich.

In line with the federal tradition of his time Mornay postulated a twofold covenant but gave it a distinctively different political twist: "The first, between God, the king, and the people that the people will be God's people; the second, between the king and the people that, if he be a proper ruler, he will be obeyed accordingly."[13]

Mornay's first question concerned the political significance of the first of these covenants. Must subjects, he asked, obey rulers whose orders contradicted the law of God? His answer was a decisive negative.

In his discussion he spelled out his concept of the covenant and affirmed its unity. "Just as the Gospels succeeded the Law," he wrote, "Christian rulers have replaced the Jewish kings. The covenant remains the same; the stipulations are unaltered; and there are the same penalties if these are not fulfilled." The conditions of the covenant—love of God and the neighbor—were, according to Mornay, stated in the Decalogue.[14]

Mornay's second question was also concerned with this basic covenant among God, the people, and the king. Could a ruler who violated God's covenant, that is, broke the law and desolated the church, be actively resisted? His answer was a decisive affirmative.

God had made the covenant with the entire community, with the people under the rule of the king. The king and the people, as a corporate body acting as a single entity, had obligated themselves within this covenant. It was the king's covenanted responsibility to ensure that the people kept the covenant. It was the covenanted obligation of the people to see that the king kept the covenant. Thus, just as it was the king's duty to maintain the law and punish offenders, there was a duty to resist the king if he proved unfaithful to the covenant and broke God's law. It was the special duty of the magistrates who occupied positions less than those of the chief magistrate or king to keep watch over the ruler and to resist him if he failed to keep the covenant.[15] Mornay went even farther. The magistrates were failing to keep the covenant if they did not resist an unjust ruler. "We have shown," he wrote, "that the people as a whole, or the officers of the kingdom whom the people have established, . . . very gravely sin against the covenant with God if they do not use force against a king who corrupts God's law or prevents its restoration, in order to confine him to his proper bounds."[16]

The third central question Mornay raised concerned the second covenant, the covenant between the king and the people.

Could a ruler be resisted who oppressed or devastated a commonwealth? Again, his answer was a resounding affirmative.

Mornay's argument for this view rested on the sovereignty of the people within a federal framework. He wrote, "And now we say that it is the people that establishes kings, gives them kingdoms, and approves their selection by its vote. For God willed that every bit of authority held by kings should come from the people, after Him, so that kings would concentrate all their care, energy, and thought upon the people's interests."[17] Mornay gave examples of the people confirming kings in the Old Testament and referred to the customary election of kings in early France. By this means, Mornay arrived at the conclusion that the people as a federated (covenanted) whole, represented by lesser magistrates, was greater than the king. The people established a ruler to be the guardian of justice and law. The king, therefore, was not above the law but was its servant.[18]

Mornay then proceeded to place his argument even more specifically within the federal framework. In the political covenant between the king and the people, he taught, the king made an absolute promise to the people to rule according to justice and law. The people promised to obey the king as long as he ruled justly. Theirs was thus a conditional promise. All legitimate government rested on such a compact, whether explicit or implicit, Mornay held. A ruler who governed contrary to justice and equity, one who violated the compact "willfully and persistently," was a tyrant and had to be resisted. The lesser magistrates or the notables of the kingdom, as federal representatives of the whole people, were obligated to resist a ruler who transgressed the covenant.[19]

Though Mornay offered no fully articulated political philosophy, he did add substantially to the emerging federal view of God, government, and people. In direct and unmistakable fashion, he stated the priority of the people over the ruler within the covenant of God and drew the conclusion that the people, through their representatives, have the right, indeed the responsibility, to resist and, if necessary, replace rulers who are unfaithful to their obligations within the societal covenant of God. Further, Mornay made clear the interwoven connectedness between faith in God, as reflected in his Reformed theology, and the social, political covenant that was the basis of government and shaped its form and the obligations of ruler and people. It remained for Althusius to build on the development of federalism within the Reformed tradition, of which Mornay is an important element, and provide the first systematic articulation of a federal political philosophy.

Johannes Althusius and the First Federal
Political Philosophy

In the archives and in the university library of the city-state of Bremen is a manuscript on federal government. It was written by Heinrich Kreffting (1562–1611), who was then chief magistrate of Bremen, in 1601. Lest some wandering scholar in the future come across this work of Kreffting's and claim that he rather than Althusius wrote the first federal political philosophy, it needs to be made clear that Kreffting provided "A Description of the Government of Bremen," not a systematic treatise on government. It does, however, provide evidence of the increasing incidence of the practice of federalism in government during the sixteenth century. Federal political philosophy did not have to be invented. It was widely practiced, especially in areas influenced by the Reformed tradition coming from Zurich and Bullinger. Althusius could draw, therefore, on many actual examples of operating federal polities as well as scholarly treatises of the past and present on government.

Long neglected in Europe and America, and at times seemingly forgotten totally, the thought of Johannes Althusius (1557?–1638) has been given renewed attention in recent decades and may be returning as a primary focus of study among historians of political thought. The federal political philosophy, to which Althusius gave the first systematic exposition, has been widely influential in shaping the patterns of government and society within and among the nations of the modern world. Carl J. Friedrich, a distinguished political philosopher and historian of the twentieth century, has called federalism the fastest growing political system of this century[20] and brought out an edition of Althusius's *Politics* with a superb introduction.[21] The careful study of this seminal figure and an appraisal of his significance for federalism over the centuries are long overdue.

Life and Work. Little is known with certainty about the early life of Althusius. He was probably born in 1557 in Diedenshausen, in what was then the domain of the counts of Wittgenstein-Berleburg. After study in Cologne in 1581, he went to Basel and completed work for a doctorate in civil and ecclesiastical law in 1586. While there, he not only became familiar with the major movements of political philosophy in the ancient world and in his own time but also concerned himself with the study of theology and with the federalism of the Reformed community of which he was a devout member. In Basel he took meals at the home of Johann Jacob Grynaeus

and perhaps resided there. Grynaeus was a distinguished Reformed theologian of federal persuasion. Althusius studied
theology and history with Grynaeus, who made a great impression on the young scholar. Althusius kept in touch with
Grynaeus until the latter's death and expressed his gratitude
for the friendship of the older man and for all that he had
learned from him.[22]

Althusius wrote his doctoral thesis on *The Succession of the
Intestate*, a subject with close relations to the issues of federal
theology. Shortly thereafter he published a treatise on Roman
jurisprudence, a work that shows the strong influence upon
him of the philosophy of Peter Ramus.[23] Almost immediately
he was called to a professorial position at Herborn, which, since
its founding in 1584 by Johann of Nassau-Orange, with Olevianus as its rector, had become a center of federal thought. It
seems likely that Althusius had already had contact with some
of the federalists who taught there, perhaps through connections made possible by Grynaeus. In any event, by Christmas of
1586 Althusius was in Herborn ready to begin teaching. Althusius was not a theologian in the sense that a specialized scholar
in theology deserves the name. Indeed, he worked in political
philosophy with the intention of establishing politics on a basis
that was independent of theology. He was, nevertheless, immersed in the federal tradition and demonstrated throughout
his writings that he had internalized this perspective. There is
evidence that he continued his study of theology while at
Herborn and also went to Heidelberg to hear lectures.[24] His
knowledge in theological studies is demonstrated also in his
extensive use of Scripture as a resource in political thought and
in his frequent references to theological works.

In spite of involving himself in a variety of civic activities and
serving a term as rector of the Herborn Academy, Althusius
published *De civile conversatione*, a treatise on ethics, in 1601,
and completed his greatest work, the *Politics*, in 1603. It received immediate and widespread attention. As a result he was
called to become syndic, or chief magistrate, of the city-state of
Emden in the northwest corner of Germany, near the Dutch
border and the North Sea. He remained in this position until
his death in 1638, providing through the years skillful leadership both in domestic affairs and in foreign relations for
Emden.[25] Two revised and enlarged editions of the *Politics* were
published during the decade after he went to Emden, one in
1610 and the other in 1614. In addition, he wrote the *Dicaiologi-
cae*, published in 1618. In his massive work, Althusius sought to
combine biblical, Roman, and common law and set forth a

triadic methodology utilizing faith, reason, and experience as parallel to his major sources and as the means for bringing them together. Always a devout Christian of Reformed faith, Althusius, from 1618 until his death, served as an elder in the Reformed church of Emden, giving no less important leadership in ecclesiastical matters than in civil government.

A Summary of Federal Thought

Inasmuch as federalism plays a central role in the political philosophy of Althusius, a brief review of the main elements of federalism as it had developed up to and including Olevianus will be helpful.

First, for the federalists, the created order is based on the covenant of God, so that the divine commandments permeate the nature of things. Federalism, therefore, has its *lex naturae* in a manner similar to what can be found in the scholastic tradition. But this moral order in creation derives from the faithful will of God in covenant, not from some rational or natural rigidity at the core of reality.

Second, human beings are created in covenant with God, subject to the divine moral order. Human society is also based on covenant, the covenant of God and human response to God in the covenants that provide the basis of all social groups. As Althusius will assert explicitly, humans are symbiotic beings by their covenantal nature, not separate individuals. There is a symbiosis between God and humanity, between humanity and creation, and among humans in community.

Third, the moral order in creation, rooted in God's covenant, permeates politics and government no less than family, church, economic relations, and all aspects of society. The social order in general and the political order in particular are covenantal or federal as the moral shape of creation emerges in human relationships.

Fourth, in human community, particular persons become representative of an entire social group. Adam, for example, is the representative of the human race in creation, in his disobedience, and in the fall into sin. Christ is the representative of the human race in redemption, in obedience, and in salvation. Thus, in all forms of social organization, for the federal perspective, there are representative humans who function as the head of a social unit and whose actions are actions of the entire group, whether family or guild, city or province, church or kingdom. This concept of representation is central both for federal theology and for federal political philosophy.

Fifth, though created within God's covenant, humans have fallen into sin. Social organization and processes must take this into account. Power exercised by humans must be limited, because that power will be used in part sinfully. Whatever virtue can be achieved in human communities depends upon patterns of checks and balances that restrain evil and incline humans toward the good that can be found in such social goals as justice and well-being but is to be found finally in God.

Sixth, the faithful activity of God in covenant does not cease with the creation of the world but continues in human community and history until the consummation of all things. Humans living in symbiotic interdependence with one another and God are constantly acting not only in response to the immediate context of other humans in the various covenants of society but also in response to the continuing activity of God the faithful One. The hope for societal justice as well as for salvation rests, for the federalists, penultimately upon the actions of humans but ultimately upon the will and action of God.

The Sources of Althusius's Thought

Whether one examines the life of Althusius or examines his writing, it is clear that the primary resource he draws on for his thought is the federal tradition of the Reformed community of faith. Otto von Gierke, among the greatest Althusian scholars, pointed out that the dominant characteristic of the political system of Althusius is its federalism.[26] Althusius is immersed in Reformed faith, in the political thought of the Reformed communities, and in biblical and theological scholarship of the Reformed tradition. The sector of that tradition that influenced him most deeply is the distinctively federal stream of thought. In no way can the centrality of the covenantal perspective for him be taken to mean that his scholarship did not range widely in historical and contemporary materials. On the contrary, the number of authors quoted in his writings and the depth of his knowledge of a great diversity of political thinkers are impressive. Yet all of his learning is shaped by the federal understanding of God, humanity, and political order.

The second resource on which Althusius draws is the Bible. For him, the Bible is not only the scripture of the Christian community and the locus of Christian faith, theology, and ethics. The Bible is also a book of political philosophy. Althusius quotes the Bible and makes extensive use of it in his *Politics*. While at Herborn, Althusius became involved in a controversy with some of the theologians. They apparently regarded it as

their exclusive prerogative to interpret the Bible, while Althusius affirmed his right to deal with Scripture and, further,
maintained that the Bible is a crucial source of political thought
and that political science would become a mongrel subject
without it.[27]

A third resource is the array of historians and political
philosophers from the ancient world with whom he is acquainted and on whom he draws in articulating his federal political
thought. Though he quotes them far less frequently than he
quotes the Bible, the writers of the ancient world form an
important part of his background. Of this group, Aristotle is
referred to most often, with Plato and Cicero falling next in
line. While making use of these authors of antiquity, Althusius
has many disagreements with them, most obviously on what
constitutes the good life for humans.[28] It must be remembered,
as Friedrich notes, "Neither Plato nor Aristotle, nor the many
political writers following in their footsteps in classical antiquity,
including the Stoics, developed a concept of federalism. This
failure is as striking as the more frequently mentioned failure
to elaborate the notion of representation."[29]

A fourth area that Althusius drew on was Roman law. While
still in Basel, just after he had completed his doctorate, Althusius published a treatise on Roman law. He had, therefore,
careful and extensive acquaintance with this tradition of jurisprudence. Throughout his *Politics*, he made frequent references to Roman law. As Friedrich points out, however, he did
not replicate the philosophy of Roman law but absorbed it into
his own perspective,[30] that is, into his federalism.

A fifth resource for Althusius were writers and controversies
of his own time. One group of writers falling into this category
were those who developed the notion of the right of the people
to resist tyrants. Mornay and the *Vindiciae contra tyrannos*, which
Althusius referred to repeatedly, provide an example already
dealt with above. There were others of the group, some from
the Reformed tradition and some from other traditions. An
important controversy during that era was over the locus of
political sovereignty. Jean Bodin (1530–1596), writing against
resistance to rulers, had defended the absolute right of kings
and affirmed that sovereignty requires centralized absolutism.
In many ways, Althusius can be seen as writing his *Politics* with
Bodin as his main opponent and with the clear intention of
drawing together into a coherent whole the varied views of
those favoring resistance. The context of contemporary controversy provided an important force shaping the federalism of
Althusius.[31]

A sixth resource was the experience with federal political structures that was emerging in the sixteenth century. When one remembers Althusius's triad of faith, reason, and experience, it is not surprising to find him drawing on the actual political practice that he discovered around him and in which he played a very active role as syndic of Emden. The formation of the United Provinces of the Netherlands in 1579, after the successful revolt against Spanish tyranny, provided a major contemporary example. The Swiss Confederation, the medieval compacts for defense and commerce such as the Hanseatic League, and the various covenants of the Greeks and the Hebrews offered additional examples. Althusius is not an armchair theoretician but combines learning with practical experience in political affairs in ways that give a distinctive texture to his political philosophy.

Basic Elements of the Political Philosophy of Althusius

After it becomes clear that the core of Althusius's thought is the covenant, with the federal perspective permeating all aspects of his politics, the other elements fall into place. His distinctive understanding of politics and its function in human society comes into focus. The various levels of social groups fall into place within the covenant. Althusius's federalism also provides insight into human nature. One of the most original elements in his thought is his view of sovereignty, forged in opposition to the centralized notion of sovereignty held by Bodin. And his articulation of the relation among covenant, revolution, and change builds on Mornay's *Vindiciae* and other similar sources, yet offers a more comprehensive perspective than his predecessors.

The Covenantal Core. The nature of politics and political association is understood and articulated by Althusius through the root metaphor of covenant. As Friedrich explains, "What Althusius undertook to do was to interpret all political life in terms of *pactum*, the bond of contractual union," or covenant.[32]

"Politics," Althusius begins, "is the art of linking humans together in order to establish, develop, and conserve social life among them. For this reason, it is called symbiotics. The content of politics, therefore, is association, in which the symbiotes make covenant with one another, either explicitly or tacitly, to a mutual sharing of whatever things are useful and necessary for harmony and productive activity in social life" (*Politics*, I, 1–2). Politics for Althusius was based on the covenanted linking of people in

symbiotic relationship, bound together in social existence, focused on a common purpose, and committed to a mutuality of
interaction that would enhance their life together. The covenant
and its agreements may be either explicit or implicit. As people
come to increasing self-awareness in society, the implicit covenants that shaped them may become more explicit. In any case,
humans, or symbiotes, are committed to one another in covenants that establish, build, and sustain society.

Althusius understands politics primarily as dealing with the
relations of humans in society. Law is not to be ignored, but it is
secondary, because it emerges from and is the product of the
context of relations shaped by the web of commitments that is
the covenant. And though Althusius is assuming that the covenant of God in creation infuses the entire world with moral
order, this order cannot be identified with a Stoic/scholastic law
of nature, which societal law must seek to replicate. The reality
of humans responding to God in the covenants of human
community provides the focus of politics rather than some
rational system.[33]

To put the point differently, the function of politics is not to
produce a well-ordered state based on natural law but rather to
find what is useful and effective in building and nurturing
community toward the fulfillment of human life and destiny. If
it appears at times that Althusius has much in common with
Aristotle, it must be remembered that their very divergent
worldviews—the biblical, Reformed faith of Althusius and the
Hellenic eudaemonistic teleology of Aristotle—give even their
apparent agreements quite different meanings.

Politics serves the function also of utilizing the varied gifts of
humans for the benefit of all. Humans are created in covenant
by God as social and political beings. In creation, abilities and
skills are distributed unevenly among humans so that they need
each other and are bound together by this mutual need. Out of
this situation arises the necessity for sharing and communicat-
ing about what is useful for the entire community. "Thus God
willed that everyone would need the abilities and aid of other
people in order that friendship would bind all together and
none could consider others to be without value. . . . All therefore have need of the interchange with and the service of other
humans, and no humans live for themselves alone (1 Cor. 10)"
(*Politics*, I, 26–27).

For political bonding, the efficient cause is the covenant as
the agreement and commitment among the citizens. The formal cause of political community is the covenant as creating the
association in which humans contribute to and communicate

with one another to establish, nurture, continue, and sustain that community which is useful and necessary for life in society (*Politics*, I, 29). The final cause of political existence is the covenant as peace, piety, and justice in a society in which humans can serve and worship God in quietude and without error (*Politics*, I, 30).

There are two basic modes of social, symbiotic association among humans. The first is simple and private. The second is mixed and public. Both modes are constituted by covenant.

The most important simple and private social group, the family, is a natural association and "a society and symbiosis initiated by a special covenant among the members for the purpose of bringing together and holding in common a particular interest" (*Politics*, II, 2).[34] The collegium or voluntary association is another social group, based on covenant, that is organized by persons for some common, useful purpose. It can last as long as the covenant partners want it and can be disbanded by their agreement. The collegia may be made of bakers, tailors, builders, merchants, philosophers, theologians, government officials, or whatever group wishes to organize for the better functioning of social life. Althusius regards these voluntary associations as important for the enhancement of symbiotic existence and devotes considerable space to describing their formation and operation (*Politics*, IV).

The covenant is the basis also of a political-civil society. Society develops from private to public associations as smaller societies unite by covenant into larger social entities—the city, the province, the commonwealth (*Politics*, V, 1–2). The smaller groups are represented in the larger group by persons who represent collectively the members of the groups from which they come, and it is the groups they represent rather than they themselves who are the members of the larger group (*Politics*, V, 9–10). If humans are gathered together without a covenant and without symbiotically affirmed rights, there is only a crowd, a mob, a collection of beings (*Politics*, V, 4).

The Covenant and Levels of Society. In contrast to political thinkers who focus only on the centralized authority of the state or only on the individual as the basic unit of society, Althusius articulates a political structure that rejects the dichotomy between the individual and the social whole and articulates a political structure with increasingly comprehensive levels. He affirms the federal principle that the insight for deciding issues on each level belongs most appropriately to those in the covenanted group at that level.

Humans as symbiotes belong by nature to families as the most immediate and basic covenantal grouping. But people also form many kinds of private associations through agreement and compact—craft guilds, academic societies, businesses and commercial associations, professional groupings, and so forth. The town or city as a political order comes into being as families and other private associations come together by covenant to form a more comprehensive symbiotic group that acts through representatives to govern and make laws. This community rests upon the consent of the private associations who participate in the covenant that is its foundation. Towns, villages, and cities may then join in covenant to form a more comprehensive association known as the province. And a covenant of provinces provides the foundation of a commonwealth. In each case, a covenant creates the more comprehensive level of political order. But the more inclusive entity does not negate the significance, participation, and consent of the covenanted groups that comprise it. Each level retains its importance and its integrity as an operative community with appropriate governmental functions.

This aspect of federalism, which plays a central role in the thought of Althusius, is known usually as the division of powers. It is one of the most distinctive and effective aspects of a federal government. In one way, it helps to assure that decisions are made and affairs governed at a level close to the persons, issues, and circumstances involved—larger issues at a more comprehensive level and local issues at a less comprehensive level. In another way, the division of powers in a federal order serves to check and balance the power of each covenanted entity and each level of comprehensiveness. The less comprehensive levels of community are limited and held in check against the misuse of power by peer groups and the commitments made to more comprehensive levels of political order. The more comprehensive levels are limited and their misuse of power checked by the controlling participation of the member groups comprising it.

At any level of society, the covenants forming each group and the covenants by which groups united into larger groups are crucial. In a commonwealth, the fundamental law of the realm is nothing else than the specific covenants through which the cities and provinces have united themselves to establish a commonwealth and to defend and enhance it by common work, counsel, and assistance (*Politics*, XIX, 49).

Human Nature.   Not only society with its various levels of federation and order but also human beings in their inmost nature are understood by Althusius in federal perspective. Humans can never be regarded as separable individuals. They are symbiotes, created by God in covenantal interdependency, interaction, and societal agreements. Such covenantal symbiosis provides the basis and the goal of political order (*Politics*, I, 3–4).

Friedrich sees the notion of symbiosis as one of the most original and durable contributions of Althusius to political thought. After extensive investigation, Friedrich comes to the conclusion that the term had not been used previously in any political writing. Althusius appears to become even more convinced that this term is appropriate for describing the social, covenantal nature of humans. The term is used in the first edition of the *Politics* but is used much more extensively in the second and third editions.[35] Power in its varied forms emerges from humans living together in symbiotic association. The notion of symbiosis also emphasizes the biological, natural basis of human nature and political order, while at the same time affirming the primacy of interaction within covenanted groups for what is distinctively human about human nature.

This fundamentally covenantal, symbiotic human nature is inevitably social. And humans find their fulfillment in the family, voluntary groups, religious associations, and political entities as federally ordered.

Sovereignty. Even more original and influential perhaps than his introduction of the notion of symbiosis into political philosophy is the way Althusius reformulates the doctrine of sovereignty. Von Gierke articulated most directly the view that Althusius took over the absolutistic conception of sovereignty put forward by Bodin and reformulated it into a powerful conception of peoples' sovereignty. "He first enunciated the proclamation of the sovereignty of the people."[36]

It is crucial, however, to note that Althusius's view of sovereignty is formulated within the root metaphor of covenant, that is, federally. The union of the people in community that provides the basis of his view is more than a social contract; it is a covenant emerging from creation, from human nature, and from the implicit and explicit agreements that provide the cumulative fabric of social order.

If the *Politics* can be said to have been directed against any political doctrine, it is the notion that sovereignty can only be vested in the king or chief magistrate. And Bodin was the most influential advocate of that position in the time of Althusius. In the preface to the first edition of the *Politics*, Althusius wrote:

I have assigned the rights of sovereignty and their sources, as I have said, to politics. But I have therein attributed them to the realm, or to the commonwealth and people. I know that in the common opinion of teachers they are to be described as belonging to the prince and supreme magistrate. Bodin clamours that these rights of sovereignty cannot be attributed to the realm or the people because they come to an end and pass away when they are communicated among subjects or the people. He says that these rights are proper and essential to the person of the supreme magistrate or prince to such a degree—and are connected so inseparably with him—that outside of his person they cease to exist, nor can they reside in any other person. . . . I maintain the exact opposite, namely, that these rights of sovereignty, as they are called, are proper to the realm to such a degree that they belong to it alone, and that they are the vital spirit, soul, heart, and life by which, when they are sound, the commonwealth lives, and without which the commonwealth crumbles and dies. . . .

I concede that the prince or supreme magistrate is the steward, administrator, and overseer of these rights. But I maintain that their ownership and usufruct properly belong to the total realm or people. . . . Their administration, which had been granted to a prince by a precarium or covenant, is returned on his death to the people. . . . This administration is then entrusted by the people to another.[37]

Sovereignty belongs to the covenanted society, to the people symbiotically united for the cultivation of what is useful for piety and justice. Such a society has political structure, with provision for a government and chief magistrate to execute the laws and to seek the welfare of all. It is not a collection of individuals but a covenanted whole that has the rights of sovereignty so that, as Althusius said in the preface to the third edition of the *Politics*, "the owner and usufructary of sovereignty is none other than the total people associated in one symbiotic body from many smaller associations."[38]

It was the duty of the supreme magistrate to administer the law, which was God's will for humans. The moral law, or the "common law," was found in the Decalogue, which informed humans about their duty to God and to their symbiotic neighbor. "Proper law" was made by the magistrate on the basis of "common law." "Proper law" was subject to change, but it had to be in agreement with "common law." Common law was generalized law; "proper law" made the precepts of the Decalogue specific for each commonwealth and specified the punishments for breaking this law. This allowed Althusius to distinguish between the Decalogue, which was "common law," and the Jewish judicial law, which was "proper law" and thus not germane to Christians.

The supreme magistrate was bound to administer laws covering both tables of the Decalogue. In other words, the magistrate cared for and made laws concerning ecclesiastical functions in the political realm. (Although Althusius's teaching resembled Bullinger's here, Althusius drew a clearer line between church and state.) Althusius spoke of a religious covenant by which the magistrate, along with his people, promised to maintain and defend the orthodox religion and the correct worship of God. This was the responsibility of the entire people, represented by the ministers, the ephors, and the supreme magistrate. The ephors had the duty to resist a magistrate who failed in his duty. This chapter in the *Politics* was a restatement of the second question of Mornay's *Vindiciae*, which is cited numerous times.

Revolution and Change. What is equally clear about the covenanted society and the sovereignty of the people is that both are founded upon the covenant of God that has infused moral order into creation and human nature. On a level more comprehensive than the political realm, there is a compact similar to but not identical with the divine and natural law of scholasticism. Political sovereignty, in the federal meaning of Althusius, is therefore not absolute. The covenants of humanity exist within the covenant of God.

Because all are bound within human covenants to the covenant of God, rulers who administer the sovereignty belonging to the people lose their authority when they violate their covenant with the people, by virtue of which they rule, or transgress the covenant of God. They are legitimate representatives of the people and have the right to administer the government only so long as they are faithful to these covenants. Intermediate officials or magistrates, called ephors by Althusius, are bound in covenant to hold chief magistrates accountable and to remove them from office if they persist in violating the covenant.

The federal political philosophy thus makes room for resisting tyrants and for revolution. Even more, Althusian federalism, drawing on Mornay and often citing the *Vindiciae*, makes it clear that the ephors are responsible for overthrow of a ruler who acts against the covenant of the people or the covenant of God. This understanding of revolution, however, is on behalf of the political and societal order rather than being designed to destroy government and replace it.

Althusius is carrying forward the teaching of the federal tradition calling for resistance to tyrants. He gives the matter a more careful articulation than it had received previously and provides a context of peoples' sovereignty and methods for limiting and removing the chief magistrate. In so doing, he formulates what can be called the notion of "federal revolution," which has been widely influential and practiced in the modern world, in contrast to the conventional notion of revolution today that is necessarily violent and rends the fabric of society with radical change.

Federal revolution can be seen, for example, in the English Revolution of 1688, in the American Revolution of 1776 to 1783, and in numerous internal changes that take place frequently in federal societies. Hannah Arendt makes the distinction in terms of types of revolutions without using the terminology we have suggested. She says that those who have carried out the middle-class revolutions in Europe and America have, for the most part, done so in ways that brought about change but carefully left the way open for further change. The violent, proletarian revolutions have produced more dramatic changes immediately but have tended to close the door to further change.[39]

In this brief sketch of Althusius's federal political philosophy, we have seen how he builds upon the long tradition of ancient and Western political thought and especially upon the federal tradition of theology and politics. While Althusius carries forward the federalism present in Bullinger, he also offers the first systematic federal political philosophy and develops it in ways that are highly original and influential. So many of the formulations of Althusius have been absorbed into the thought of subsequent political philosophers and into the practice of modern federal societies that it is easy to overlook the significance of this seminal federalist who has done much to shape republican-democratic government in the modern world.

4

The Zenith of Federal Theology: Johannes Cocceius

Usually the people contemporary with us who influence us most are not persons selected for focus by the media but those who are close to us and have cared for us in immediate and loving ways. In parallel fashion, some of the people in our past who have been most influential on our outlook are not well known. The individualistic bias that has permeated the work of many modern historians has focused on individual leaders who represent the triumph of a trend rather than the varied persons and groups that developed the movement, nurtured it before it became ascendant, and shaped the ideas to which we are heir.

Nowhere is this more apparent than in the case of the federal tradition. The culture of the modern West, most especially in the United States, is shaped by federalism. We know of George Washington and James Madison, who were crucial figures in the time of the American Revolution, the writing of the Federal Constitution, and the founding of the republic. But someone like Johannes Althusius, who built upon the past and forged the federal heritage that Washington and Madison brought to victory in the emerging United States, remains unknown.

We do not understand, however, who we are today and what we believe if we explore only our own context of thought, problems, and action. Nor do we understand the era of the writing of the Constitution well if we look only at what occupied the focal attention of the founding leaders. There is also the important tacit dimension of human living. For us, the tacit dimension is all we have inherited and presupposed that forms the accepted substructure of our patterns of thinking and acting today. The varied group who gathered in Philadelphia in May 1787 and who by September had produced one of the most remarkable political documents in the history of human government also shared a context that enabled them to accomplish their task.

This brief exploration of the federal tradition is intended to help retrieve the tacit dimension of our culture, the part of our lived patterns that is not explicitly known yet continues to permeate and shape the structures of our thinking and action. Heinrich Bullinger's treatise *The Covenant* has been lifted up as the fountainhead of the federal tradition. We have traced briefly the influence of Bullinger and this seminal work and in the process pointed to some of the individuals who nourished and contributed to the development of federalism. One of these was Johannes Althusius, whose work in formulating federal political philosophy we examined in the previous chapter. Now we turn to a thinker of the seventeenth century who is as forgotten as Althusius but who provided the most comprehensive expression of the federal theology, Johannes Cocceius of Bremen. His presentation of federalism helped make it so pervasive that we presuppose his ideas rather than notice them.

Federal Theology, from Herborn to Bremen

Of all the galaxy of federal thinkers who taught at Herborn, who made it into one of the most important centers of federalism in Europe, and who were colleagues of Althusius's, none stands out more clearly than Matthias Martini. He provides the strong connection between Herborn federalism and its brilliant expression in the thought of Cocceius.

Born in Freienhagen in Waldeck, Matthias Martini (1572–1630) received his education in his home community and at Herborn. In 1595, he became the court preacher in Nassau-Dillenburg and, the following year, professor in the Herborn Academy. As such, he would have been in close association, not only with the federal theologians there, but also with the professor of jurisprudence, Johannes Althusius. Indeed, while teaching there, he became involved in a dispute with Althusius concerning whether theologians or magistrates had the authority to distinguish between what was temporal and what was eternal in the Bible. Martini was joined by his colleagues in theology, Johannes Piscator and Wilhelm Zepper. The disagreement was settled amicably, though Althusius refused to yield interpretation of Scripture exclusively to theologians and continued to maintain that the Bible occupies a central place in political science.[1]

Because of his connection with Althusius, Martini left Herborn in 1607 to become pastor of the Reformed church in

Emden, where Althusius had gone in 1604 to become syndic. In 1610, Martini accepted a call to become professor of sacred philology and rector at the Gymnasium Illustre in Bremen. He spent the remaining twenty years of his life there, attracting by his learning and personality pupils from many parts of Germany as well as from Switzerland, Hungary, Denmark, Norway, Scotland, France, Spain, and especially from the nobility of Bohemia and Moravia.[2] However, his most brilliant and influential student, Johannes Cocceius, came from the city of Bremen itself.

Covenant thought had already played an important role in the theology of Bremen prior to Martini. In 1595, Urban Pierius had published a treatise with the title, translated into English, "Sixty-two Aphorisms Concerning the Covenant of God with Humanity." In this work, federal principles provide the basis for the theology set forth. Heppe adds that the federal theology was "cultivated with special zeal" in Bremen.[3]

Martini was an accomplished biblical and theological scholar and a prolific writer.[4] His theological thought appeared most concisely in a short work published in 1618 entitled "Concerning the Signs of the Covenants of Nature and Grace" as well as, in somewhat longer form, in his *Summa theologiae*, a collection of public disputations that Martini gave on various theological topics before the students and faculty in Bremen.

As might be expected from his educational background in Herborn and his acceptance in Bremen, Martini's theology was federal in structure, with a distinction between the covenant of nature, which God had concluded with Adam before the fall, and the covenant of grace with the faithful, which Christ sealed with his death. The covenant of grace had the three economies noted in prior federalists—before the law, under the law, and after the law, in Christ. Jesus Christ was, for Martini, the center of the covenant of grace in all three economies, implicitly in the earlier two and explicitly in the consummating phase. From this federal core, the covenant was developed so that it pervaded all other elements of Martini's thought. With reference to predestination, he held to a moderate Reformed view consistent with his federal convictions.

The moderation of his Reformed federalism was put to a severe test on an international level when the controversy in the Netherlands between the Remonstrants and the high Calvinists there drew all Reformed communities of Europe into its orbit. The turmoil in Holland came to intense focus at the Synod of Dort in 1618–1619. The Dutch leaders requested representatives from the Reformed churches in other countries, and most of them complied by sending delegations. Martini was one of those representing the Bremen church.

The controversy that gave rise to the Synod of Dort emerged in the last decade of the sixteenth century as the high Calvinist position on predestination acquired greater rigidity and gained influence in the Netherlands. Jacobus Arminius, a Reformed minister in Amsterdam who had studied in Geneva, took the position that high predestinarianism went beyond what could be found in Scripture and tended to render human responsibility meaningless. Appointed a professor of theology in the University of Leiden in 1602, a post for which he would have been unacceptable had his view been judged at that time to go beyond the bounds of Reformed orthodoxy, Arminius soon came under attack from Franciscus Gomarus, already a professor at Leiden and a leader of the growing rigid faction in the Dutch church.

To support his views, Gomarus appealed beyond the Bible to contemporary opinion. "Church doctrine," he affirmed, "does not consist merely of accepted creeds, but also in the unanimous view of the preachers." Johannes Bogermann, a high Calvinist who later would preside over the Synod of Dort, asserted that Scripture must be interpreted according to the Catechism and the Confession rather than those statements according to the Bible. Arminius, on the other hand, held that Scripture must have priority over creeds and contemporary opinion.

From the university lecture halls, the dispute spread into the churches, into the marketplace, and into the political arena. The theological issues became intertwined with the tension between John Oldenbarnevelt, prime minister of the United Provinces and leader of the political group favoring republican government, and Prince Maurice, the stadtholder who headed the army and the political group favoring monarchy. The emerging conflict also set the middle-class merchants, who were republican in political sentiments, against the landed nobility and peasants, who were monarchist.

After the death of Arminius in 1609, the theological leadership of the movement passed into less careful doctrinal hands. The Five Articles of the Remonstrants, developed in 1610 in opposition to the growing power of the high Calvinists, posed the issues too sharply and tended to drive the moderates in the churches into alliance with the high party.[5]

Prince Maurice, son and heir of William of Orange, at first tried to steer clear of the religious controversy, saying, "I am a soldier, not a divine." Later, however, as Oldenbarnevelt, a hero of the struggle against Spain, became aligned with the Remonstrants, as the Arminian party came to be designated, Maurice shifted his position and was reported as saying, "I know nothing of predestination, whether it is green or whether it is blue; but I do know that Oldenbarnevelt's pipe and mine will never play the same tune."[6]

In 1617, as the intensity of the conflict escalated and the Synod of Dort loomed ahead, Prince Maurice used the military forces under his command to carry out a bloodless coup. Troops went from city to city and deposed any council members with Remonstrant-republican loyalties and replaced them with persons of high Calvinist–monarchist views. Accusations of disloyalty to the Netherlands and treasonous dealings with Spain were made against the Remonstrant-republicans, even against the aged Prime Minister Oldenbarnevelt, who had done more than anyone except William of Orange himself to secure the freedom of the Dutch from Spain.[7]

With the opposition eliminated, delegates to Dort were selected and the synod convened, thoroughly in control of the high Calvinists and monarchists. There were, however, delegates from other Reformed churches present. In spite of the skewed composition of the synod in its representation from the Dutch churches, the rigid predestinarian faction did not emerge with a total victory. The Articles of the Remonstrance were condemned. Anything less would have meant total triumph for those who had been ejected by armed force and brought to trial. Supralapsarianism, the cornerstone of the high Calvinist position, was not affirmed. The way was left open in the carefully worded article on the subject for supralapsarian and infralapsarian views, indicating the influence of the moderates. It was probably the presence of the foreign delegations that led to the temperate outcome. Among those leading the moderate forces at Dort were Matthias Martini and Ludwig Crocius, the representatives from Bremen.

The political triumph of the high Calvinist–monarchist faction was more complete. On the domestic politics, the foreign delegations had little influence. At the conclusion of the Synod of Dort, Oldenbarnevelt, who had devoted his life to the cause of Dutch freedom, was executed in the public square. In Dutch political history, Dort became a scene of monumental shame and tragedy.

Even with its theological conclusions much less than the high party had sought, the influence of Dort was limited and its affirmations were dubious as representing the mainstream of the Reformed tradition. The English delegates declined to sign

the Canons of Dort, and the Church of England, with its strong
Reformed tendencies, explicitly rejected the synod's decrees. It
is far from clear that the Swiss churches endorsed the results.
The French and German Reformed churches refused to be
guided by the results of Dort, and the representatives of
Bremen and Hesse expressed direct disagreement with some of
the conclusions reached.[8] Even in the Netherlands a more
moderate theological and political temper prevailed than that
controlling the dominant Dutch sector of the assembly. As one
historian has observed, "The Synod's demand that confession
of the Dordrecht doctrine be made a condition for appoint-
ment to government office was never conceded by the secular
authorities. Petition after petition to that effect was coolly
ignored by the merchant rulers."[9]

The basis of Martini's opposition to the high Calvinist views
dominant among the Dutch delegates to Dort was his Reformed
faith, coming from Bullinger through Herborn to Bremen. For
him, Scripture, through which, under the guidance of the Holy
Spirit, God is revealed, and God's covenant take precedence
over political and social pressures and even over creeds, important as they may be within the Christian church. He rejected the
view that the sovereignty of God can be derived by logical
necessity from a dogmatically formulated Eternal Decree. Predestination understood in the high, rational manner eliminated
human response and responsibility, took away the significance
of selfhood and history, and placed logic ahead of love, mercy,
and faithfulness in the understanding of God. Instead, drawing
on the biblical, juristic images of the federal tradition, Martini
viewed God as relating to the world and the human race more
through covenantal faithfulness than logical entailment, as
ruling more as a monarch or a magistrate governs a community
of citizens than as an artisan operates a machine, and calling
humans to response in faith rather than subjecting them to a
rational necessity settled before the creation of the world. As we
have seen, federal theology does not relinquish the doctrines of
God's sovereignty and predestining will but interprets these
teachings with covenantal rather than rational images having
priority. Martini incorporates this perspective in his federalism,
and it shaped his contributions to the Synod of Dort.

Martini provides an interesting and important link within the
federal stream of Reformed thought. He connects Herborn
and Bremen, both centers of federal thought. He is also closely
related to the two figures who provide the most comprehensive
formulations of federal thought in the seventeenth century—
Althusius, who published the first systematic federal political

philosophy, with whom Martini was associated in Herborn and in Emden, and Cocceius, whose work represents the zenith of federal theology and whom Martini taught in Bremen.

The Reformation and Cocceius

To understand the importance of Cocceius and his achievement, it is necessary to place him in relation to the Reformation and its central theological intention. The Reformation of the sixteenth century was, as interpreted by the movements emerging from it, a recovery of the Bible, a return to biblical Christianity, and a rejection of the medieval distortions of scriptural faith. Clearly there is much evidence to support this view. The Reformation begins in a decisive way with Martin Luther's discovery in the Epistle to the Romans of the message of justification by faith. He translated the Bible out of Latin, which few people understood, into contemporary German. This daring move, bolstered by the invention of printing, made the Bible available for widespread reading and interpretation. All elements of the emerging Protestant movement base themselves on Scripture and direct the attention of the Christian community directly to the Bible itself in a way that had not been the case for over a thousand years. While there are exceptions in the Middle Ages to the general neglect of the Bible—the Waldenses, the Lollards, the Hussites—these groups foreshadow what took place on a larger scale in the Reformation.

Even so, the past lay heavily upon the Reformers and their followers. The thought forms of medieval theology were not discarded without struggle. Scholasticism, either in its Aristotelian form or in some parallel tendency to deduce theology from dogma rather than let theology emerge from devout attention to the Bible, often remained or soon crept back into Protestant thought.

Limited knowledge of Hebrew and Greek and the historical context of Scripture was still another way that the past made it difficult to realize the intentions that inspired the Reformation. The Renaissance and humanism were powerful allies of the Reformation in helping to recover the past and in cultivating literacy and learning beyond the social elite of ecclesiastical scholars. For a time, the ability to teach the ancient languages of the Hellenic and Hebrew cultures drew crowds of students comparable to those learning computer skills in the late twentieth century.

It took time and the gradual development of new skills of language and historical learning to carry through the intent of the Reformation. There is, therefore, a sense in which the Christians of the seventeenth century were able to go more directly to the Bible than had the early adherents of various Protestant movements. The Bible of the early church was Greek, both the Old and the New Testament. The Bible of the Middle Ages was Latin. Only after the Renaissance and the Reformation had gone through development over time was it possible for the New Testament in Greek and especially the Old Testament in Hebrew to have profound influence on Christian thought. Norman Snaith raises the interesting question: "When Protestantism went back to the Hebrew Bible, did this have any effect on Protestant theology?"[10] The answer undoubtedly is a resounding yes. The course of development of federal theology, with its changes and growth from Bullinger onward, is one major effect of the recovery of the biblical languages, and most especially the recovery of Hebrew and the study of the historical context of Scripture.

Johannes Cocceius and his own remarkable expression of federalism provide an example of the fulfillment of the hopes engendered by the Reformation. The comprehensiveness that covenant thought based on the Bible achieved in his hands was possible only after biblical scholarship had developed and matured over a long period of time. The breadth of his academic training and the depth with which he cultivated biblical languages, rabbinical studies, historical scholarship, and hermeneutics produced results that enabled Gottlob Schrenk correctly to affirm: "The theological development that arose in the wake of the Reformation arrives [with Cocceius] at a decisive turning point, so that Cocceius must be designated as a momentous event in the history of Protestantism."[11]

Life and Work of Cocceius

Johannes Cocceius (1603–1669), or Koch, as the family name was spelled before Johannes and his brother Gerhard changed it to the Latin version in line with the academic custom of the time, was born in Bremen of a family old and renowned in the service of the city-state. Among his ancestors, on both his father's and his mother's side of the family, are an impressive succession of public leaders of Bremen. The family was Reformed in faith, and Cocceius was reared in a strict and devout home. One writer affirmed, with apparently unconscious humor, that "an earnestly religious and therefore industrious tone ruled the household."[12] Every free hour was devoted to work and study, with the parents taking direct charge of the religious life of the family. There was daily family worship. Church attendance and private prayer were inculcated from early childhood. In such a home, instruction in Christian faith was not neglected. The theology that he would have learned was a form of federalism, bolstered probably by Bullinger's *Hausbuch* and Hermann Ravensperger's *Wegweiser.*

Bremen had a republican, federal government. The Reformed doctrine of the Bremen church was federal theology. Cocceius was imbued with federalism from birth, whether learning about his ancestry, assisting his father in his duties as secretary to the chief magistrate of Bremen, or attending to the life of faith at home and at church.

After receiving his early schooling, the young Cocceius enrolled in the Gymnasium Illustre, where Matthias Martini was teacher and rector. Over the years during which he studied there, Cocceius formed a strong friendship with Martini, calling the older man his second father.[13] After discovering Cocceius's abilities, Martini gave personal supervision to the studies of the brilliant youth. Cocceius studied Latin, Greek, Hebrew, Chaldee, Syriac, and Arabic with Martini, the philologist and federal theologian. Encouraged by Martini, Cocceius entered upon rabbinical studies.

Though specializing in languages and sacred philology, Cocceius took the usual broad range of gymnasium studies, including physics, philosophy, and of course theology. After completing his studies in Bremen, Cocceius went to Hamburg to pursue rabbinical studies further under the guidance of Jewish scholars and to become even better versed in Hebrew and the Jewish Scriptures.

Cocceius then continued his education at the University of Franeker in order to study with Sixtinus Amama, one of the greatest Orientalists of his time. While at Franeker, he also studied with Maccovius, a Reformed scholastic theologian, and with William Ames, a Puritan covenant theologian in exile from England. Under Amama, Cocceius prepared his first published work, which brought him to the favorable attention of noted scholars elsewhere in Europe. From a base in biblical languages and the study of Scripture, Cocceius was being launched on a career as a federal theologian.

Another source of federal influence was Johannes's older brother, Gerhard (1601–1660). Gerhard was an eminent jurist and statesman, trained in jurisprudence, with a doctorate from Strassburg. In addition to teaching, he served as senator, magistrate, and ambassador for Bremen and one of its representatives to the conference that produced the Peace of Westphalia

in 1648, ending the Thirty Years War. After 1654, he taught at
the University of Groningen and was scarcely less distinguished
in his own time than Johannes. From earliest childhood, the
brothers had a close relationship that lasted throughout their
lives—Gerhard learning federal theology from Johannes and
Johannes's coming to understand God's covenantal governance
in political affairs from Gerhard.

Upon completion of his studies in Franeker, Cocceius was
called to Bremen to teach in place of Martini, who had recently
died. After teaching in Bremen from 1630 to 1636, he was
called to a chair at the University of Franeker, where he taught
from 1636 to 1650, and then became professor of theology at
Leiden, in what was perhaps the most distinguished university
in Europe at that time, and remained there until his death in
1669.

Cocceius began his career as a teacher of sacred philology in
Bremen and continued to devote himself to this field of study
in Franeker. Increasingly, however, he moved into the exegesis
of Scripture and toward explicit attention to theology. In 1643
he began occupying a double professorship, in Hebrew and in
theology. His publications, which at first had been in biblical
languages and exegesis, gradually shifted into theology. In
1648 he published his first major work in federal theology,
"Collations of Text Concerning the Covenant and Testament
of God," expanded in the edition of 1653 and retitled *Summa
doctrinae de foedere et testamento Dei.*

Cocceius, working with inflexible industry, produced lectures
and publications reflecting his exegesis of every book of the
Bible, a massive *Summa theologiae ex Sacris Scripturis repetita,* and
numerous treatises on a variety of topics, all explicating the
federal theology that he found in Scripture. In the final decade
of his life, he also completed a massive Hebrew lexicon.

Students came from all over Europe to hear him and study
with him. In particular, in this period when English dissenters
were not permitted to study in Oxford and Cambridge, Leiden
was second only to Edinburgh as the university to which they
flocked for university education. Cocceius thus became a focal
point in connecting the development of federal theology in
Germany, the Netherlands, and Great Britain.

The Federal Theology of Cocceius

When first encountered by a twentieth-century reader, the
writings of Cocceius appear forbidding and obscure, as is the case
with most academic authors of the seventeenth century. His

thought is set forth in twelve folio volumes, almost all in Latin. Little of his work has been published in English translation. Not only is it a problem of another language, the style of writing is difficult and the patterns of thought are, in many ways, unlike our own. In addition, seventeenth-century theologians could never be accused of practicing brevity and conciseness.

In spite of these barriers, the study of Cocceius can become increasingly exciting. He was embarked on a serious effort to fulfill the Reformation intention of cutting through the dogmatic accretions of the Middle Ages and attending to God's self-revelation to humanity through the Bible. As we break through the difficulties, we find Cocceius wrestling with issues that continue to face us today. And, though we shall not find his thought totally satisfying either as to style or content, he has much to teach us and can throw helpful light on the development of federalism and its significance for the modern world.

From first to last, Cocceius was a federal theologian and brought federalism to its most profound and influential formulation in theology. For Cocceius, the covenant existed prior to history within the Godhead; love, community, and faithfulness are, therefore, what Christians believe to be at the core of the divine reality.[14] From sheer grace, God made a covenant with nature in the creation of the world. This pact contained commands and promises and thus was a covenant of works between God and humanity. It was abrogated by Adam's rebellion, disobedience, and fall; in the fall, humans are placed in bondage to sin and death.[15] God then upholds the one and eternal covenant by establishing the covenant of grace that is fulfilled in Jesus Christ, demonstrating that "grace, above all, is God's will unto salvation."[16]

Within this overall federal frame, several elements of Cocceius's theology deserve special attention today. First, there is the clear intention to be a biblical theologian and the way he carries out this intention. Second, Christian theology for Cocceius arises out of the encounter of the Christian community of faith with God through the Bible rather than from philosophy. Third, the principles for interpreting Scripture, or his hermeneutics, must be noted, in part because of their influence on the development of biblical scholarship and in part for what they can teach us today. Fourth, the "historical method" of Cocceius was central to his thought, had impact on movements that have shaped the modern world, and remains important for us today. Fifth, there is the fascinating understanding of human nature that underlies the thought of Cocceius and is at the core of much of the federal tradition as it develops politically.

Biblical Theology

Cocceius intended throughout to base his theology on the revelation of God through Scripture. His federalism, therefore, was biblical theology. He believed that the appropriate concepts and language for expressing Christian faith were to be derived through the medium of the Bible. The creeds of the church were important for him, but the Bible was even more important. Yet the words of Scripture in themselves were not sufficient. The Holy Spirit had to illumine the minds of those who read and studied the Bible. Christian theology, therefore, emerged from the relationship of faith in God by means of devout attention to Scripture.[17]

It is well to remember that Cocceius came to theology through biblical languages, sacred philology, exegesis, rabbinics, and Oriental studies, what we today would include under the heading biblical studies. Only gradually did his scholarly work lead him to turn his attention directly to theology. Even as he formulated and published doctrinal works, however, he remained grounded in the study of the Bible. This is clearly demonstrated in his *Summa doctrinae de foedere et testamento Dei*, and the priority of the Bible continued to permeate all of his work. One historian has described his approach in this way:

> Cocceius based his theory of life upon the Bible, and in this lies his significance. In contradistinction to devotion to church and orthodoxy, he recommends a life in and through the Scriptures. Against Hoornbeeck's "Authority of the Church" he put that of the Bible only, which to him was a wonderful expression of the deeds and words of God.[18]

This does not mean that Cocceius rejected creeds. His expositions of the Heidelberg Catechism and the Belgic Confession affirmed their teachings and demonstrated that he adhered to them. But he insisted on the primacy of the Bible in relation to all church doctrine.

Theology Independent of Philosophy

In parallel fashion to the relation of Bible and tradition, Cocceius maintained that Christian theology was independent of philosophy and depended ultimately on revelation. Theology, he wrote, "is knowledge and speech, speech about God, from God, in the presence of God to God's own glory."[19] Theologians ought to study philosophy and make use of human rational powers, but "reason is the servant of theology, not its master."[20] He is therefore opposed to any form of scholasticism as a primary method in theology. J. A. Dorner sums up Cocceius's influence in this area as follows: "Federalism broke the rule of Aristotelian scholasticism and placed in its stead—nay, in that of dogmatics—investigation of the Scripture, and the study of the Hebrew language."[21]

Principles of Interpretation

Cocceius gave careful attention to the ways in which Scripture is to be interpreted, that is, to hermeneutics. First, as emphasized above, he held that the Word of God, revealed through Scripture and interpreted by the Holy Spirit, was the source of all sound Christian doctrine. Second, he made it clear that the Bible must be interpreted as an organic whole. Basic to his method of interpretation is the notion that the words of the Bible "mean what they can signify within their total context."[22] Third, this total context, Cocceius said, must be understood, not only as the immediate setting of a passage and its relation to the whole of Scripture, but also as the most profound understanding of biblical languages possible and the broadest range of historical and archaeological materials. Even after the superb education that Martini and others gave him at Bremen, he pursued the study of the Hebrew language with rabbis in Hamburg and sought out the great Orientalist, Sixtinus Amama, at Franeker in order to do special study with him. Fourth, interpreters must try to discover the meaning of Scripture rather than approach the Bible seeking confirmation of dogmas already held. "Interpretation of the Scripture," he wrote pointedly and succinctly, "is by exegesis, *from* Scripture, not by eisegesis, *into* Scripture."[23] Fifth, he taught that the Bible "is not of private interpretation."[24] Against any kind of individualism, he not only spoke of his own symbiotic relations within his family, his educational context, and the community of faith, but also insisted that the guidance of the Holy Spirit is available to all the faithful and that it is within the Christian community of interpretation that the message of God emerges. God alone knows the whole of the divine will, so human knowledge may be true without being adequate or complete.[25] Finally, and crucially, the center of God's revelation is Christ. The one great purpose of revelation in the Old and New Testaments is to unfold "the mystery of godliness, God manifest in the flesh."[26]

For Cocceius, the starting point of interpretation was faith in the saving revelation of God in Jesus Christ. Humans were fallen, and there could be no saving knowledge of God apart from revelation. Therefore hermeneutics not only was scholarly reasoning but required the illumination of the Holy Spirit. This illumination does not occur by accumulating proof texts. "Many people," he wrote, "put Scripture in place of the Pope. They are orthodox *a la mode.* . . . From the beginning God has spoken in figures. . . . All have understood to whom God has given eyes illumined for seeing."[27]

Cocceius is quite open to a plurality of interpretations. In affirming this he wrote:

> God is distributing gifts in divers ways. . . . There is no law that orders the person who comes after to be content with the things his predecessors have learned, thought, perceived, and explained. . . . It is good that the same things be said from the Scriptures by many mouths lest it might appear that nothing else could be learned from the Bible.[28]

From one perspective, Cocceius must be seen as laying the foundation for what will become the critical study of the Bible in the next century. His disciple Compegius Vitringa will build on the work of Cocceius and, as a twentieth-century biblical scholar asserts, employ in his *Observationes sacra* (1683) the "principle according to which characteristics of a document are induced from the observation of its contradictions, chronological allusions, literary inconsistencies, and the like."[29]

Yet Cocceius also remained within the community of faith in God, within which he believed true interpretation of the Bible can occur. Thus, from another perspective, Cocceius can be seen as fulfilling the intention of the great Reformers to base formulations of Christian faith on the Bible, interpreted through the Holy Spirit, but to do so with the biblical scholarship developed over a century and a half rather than with the new linguistic and historical tools just emerging from the Renaissance at the beginning of the sixteenth century.

Historical Method

Cocceius understood Scripture as permeated and shaped by the covenant of God. Following Bullinger, he sees the one, eternal covenant, experienced by humans in its unfolding phases or economies, as the framework of meaning in the Bible—in creation, in human fallenness, in history, in Jesus Christ, in redemption, and in the consummation of all things in God. Christian theology, therefore, must have covenant and Christ as its center and attempt to elaborate the purposes of God from creation, through the whole of history, to the end.

Whereas the high Calvinists and Reformed scholastics saw all meaning concentrated in the Eternal Decree, Cocceius emphasized the significance of God's redemptive activity in history. God is the initiator and final arbiter in this history of salvation, but human response within the context of world events also had meaning.

The message of God was, for Cocceius, revealed through the unfolding of the successive stages of the covenant as these are discovered in Scripture. The covenant is neither single nor simple but complex and developing. First, the covenant of God existed as part of the divine order, between the Father and the Son before creation. Second, the covenant is made with creation and humanity in Adam as a covenant of nature or works, which was abrogated by rebellion and unfaithfulness. Third, following the fall into sin, God established the covenant of grace with humanity, within which faith takes the place of works. Fourth, the covenant of grace unfolds toward its fulfillment in Jesus Christ.[30] The essential meaning of creation and history is understood as deriving from God's activity in the unfolding phases of the covenant. The sovereignty of God remained, and so also did the depth of historical process and human responsibility.

Human Nature

Perhaps the most fascinating aspect of Cocceius's federal theology appears in his view of human nature, which draws on the Bible and tradition but is strikingly different at certain points from the Augustinian views that have dominated much of Western thought and the modern reactions to those views. Cocceius's perspective illumines and helps explain the understanding of human nature permeating the federal political tradition and the ways that understanding differs decisively both from the Augustinian view and from the liberal reaction. The major elements of Cocceius's innovative view can be drawn from what has already been said about his theology.

First, humans are covenantal by their created nature. Covenants describe the relation between God and humanity, between humans and nature, and the symbiotic interdependence among humans. Covenants, explicitly and implicitly, characterize the social context in which humans emerge and come to awareness and self-identity.

Second, the covenant was, for Cocceius, a way of dealing with plurality and of drawing from it a sense of unitary meaning in creation, history, and faith. The will of God, or the Eternal

Decree, is understood, not in monolithic and rigidly logical fashion, but as faithful action in the Godhead and governing the unfolding of world history toward its fulfillment. The varied covenants of human society were, for him, responsive to the covenant of God and fit into the creative, ordering, and redeeming governance of God.

Third, his federal understanding of human nature regarded humans as social and sinful, both seen in terms of covenant. Parallel to Althusius, Cocceius saw humans as in symbiotic relation with God, nature, and one another. Yet, in contrast to God's faithfulness, humans are fallen into sin, understood as rebellion against God and unfaithfulness to the covenant with God and to the covenants of human society. Human knowing is, therefore, always partial and governed more by sin than covenantal justice and love.

Fourth, any virtue in human society must be seen, not as a result of human goodness, but as a social achievement resulting from the interaction of humans in covenant as God's grace works in the redeeming activity of historical process. Both the scholastic reliance on rational insight into natural law and the liberal reliance on individual virtue in social context are rejected without ignoring the function of reason or the importance of societal interaction.

Fifth, nature, history, and humanity are created in covenantal process toward an unknown future and consummation in God. In one of the most intriguing innovations of his theology, Cocceius drew out an implication of biblical federalism that had apparently not been made explicit before but made clear a central dimension of federal thought. As Cocceius put it, humans are created mutable, changeable, in process, open to the obedient love of God through which they have community with God and with one another. In the rebellion and disobedience that constitutes the fall into sin, humans become immutable, resistant to change, denying the process in which they were created that leads toward fulfillment in God.[31]

The restlessness of the human heart was not, as Augustine suggested, the result of the fall. Instead, for Cocceius, the restlessness of change was implanted with the creation of humans within the covenant of God. Neither nature nor humans are created perfect or complete. They are created incomplete, striving toward greater completeness and fulfillment in and through the covenants by which God shapes the world toward consummation.

The emphasis on change and on continuing revolutions that leave the future open to further change has characterized political federalism in a way that may seem strange unless its origins in the history of the federal tradition are known. Then the deeply implanted awareness of the governance of God emerges clearly, a governance exercised by means of a federal ordering of societal interaction that impels humanity, in spite of human sin, to seek greater justice, peace, and love. This federal view is far from a faith in automatic progress, but it does provide a basis for limited hope in the possibilities of prudent political processes.

With Cocceius and his followers, federalism becomes so generally pervasive in Reformed communities as to displace or reshape other streams of thought. It also becomes less visible because it is increasingly the common perspective within societies deeply influenced by Reformed thought. Federalism becomes the spectacles through which modern Western humans look at their world. Like fish in water, modern humanity exists in federal history and culture.

5

Federalism and the
U.S. Constitution of 1787

The great British statesman and prime minister William E. Gladstone uttered one of the most famous statements describing the Federal Constitution of the United States and the process by which it came into being. He called it "the most wonderful work ever struck off at a given time by the brain and purpose of man."[1] Americans usually note only this part of what Gladstone said, regard it as a great tribute to our founders, and are very pleased. What can easily be overlooked is that the British leader was drawing a contrast between the gradual, organic growth of the British constitution and the sudden construction of the American document. It has been taken as praise, when, in fact, there is much more of a double-edged meaning, in part tribute to the accomplishment at Philadelphia in 1787 and in part suggesting that the United States and its Constitution lack history and tradition as compared with Great Britain. In so doing, Gladstone betrays a characteristic and monumental misunderstanding by Europeans of America, a misunderstanding that Americans often share because they tend to be far too gullible about what Europeans tell them.

It is true, of course, that the Federal Constitution of the United States was written in less than four months, between late May and mid-September in the summer of 1787. It represents, however, the culmination of a long process of development in the colonial period. Almost two hundred years of political thought and experience in America lie behind those one hundred days in Philadelphia. And, in light of the brief history of federalism in the previous chapters, it becomes clear that the leaders of the British colonies in the New World, from Sir Walter Raleigh's aborted beginning on Roanoke Island, through Virginia, New England, and the Middle Colonies, on to the time of the American Revolution, were drawing on a federal tradition stretching back in specific terms to Bullinger and Zurich and in more general terms into medieval and biblical times. Gladstone was correct in praising the efforts of those who brought forth the Federal Constitution. He was speaking from a mistaken English complacency in suggesting that only the British have real traditions.

To fill in this sketch of the federalism emerging from the work of Heinrich Bullinger, illustrated especially in his treatise *The Covenant*, it will be helpful to provide a brief account of the connections between the federal tradition in Switzerland, Germany, the Netherlands, and Britain and federalism in theology and political thought as it developed in the British colonies. What occurred in the colonial period and at Philadelphia must rank as one of the most significant emanations from the fountainhead of federalism.

Federal Theology and Politics in New England

As we have seen, federal thought had by the end of the sixteenth century become pervasive in the Reformed communities of Europe. It is not surprising to discover, therefore, that federalism was brought over to the New World with the earliest settlements of people of Reformed faith. Though Puritan influence can be discerned in Virginia, the place where covenantal forms of life and thought are most pronounced is New England.

Most of the leaders of the New England colonies adhered to one or another version of federal theology and politics. Their theory is embedded in their actions and expressed in their speeches and writing. Anyone who seeks to find representatives of liberal democracy as understood in the twentieth century among the New England leaders is doomed to disappointment. If, however, one seeks earlier forms of the federalism that became embodied in the U.S. Constitution, the examples are plentiful. For these leaders, the covenant was at the same time a way of expressing the relation between God and humans and also an understanding of the appropriate political order within the divine-human covenant.

The impact of Reformed faith and federalism in Britain was primarily on three groups: first, on the Presbyterians in Scotland; second, on the Church of England, where the Reformed influence emerged gradually in the Puritan movement; and third, on the separatist Protestant groups in England. Members of this third group were the first to arrive in New England.

The Pilgrims

Though Reformed influence, especially from Zurich and Bullinger, had entered England quite early, it was after the Roman Catholic reaction under Mary Tudor had made many martyrs and forced others into exile that the Reformed impact increased greatly. Exiles who had spent time in Zurich and Geneva returned after Elizabeth succeeded to the throne and turned England again toward Protestantism. Fired with zeal, they rapidly gained converts to the movement that, by 1564, was already called "Puritan." For the most part, this Reformed, or Puritan, movement took shape within the Church of England and sought to purify it of Romish theology and practice. Part of the movement, however, went farther in its rejection of the Catholic tendencies of the Anglican Church and set up separate congregations. Thus they are called Separatists.

Persecuted by the church and government of Elizabeth, whose religious settlement permitted great breadth of belief and practice but required conformity to the basic standards of the Church of England, Separatists in great numbers fled to the Continent. Many of them settled in Amsterdam and Leiden, within the relatively tolerant atmosphere of the Dutch republic. The Leiden congregation decided to send part of its membership to America. In 1620 this group set out under the leadership of William Brewster and William Bradford, landed on the shores of Cape Cod in the late fall, and established the colony of Plymouth. This group is known as the Pilgrims.

Before landing, forty-one male passengers assembled in the main cabin of the *Mayflower*, the small vessel on which they traversed the Atlantic Ocean, and signed an agreement known as the Mayflower Compact, a "combination," as William Bradford explains in *The History of Plymouth Plantation*, "made by them before they came ashore . . . occasioned partly by the discontented and mutinous speeches that some of the strangers amongst them had let fall from them in the ship . . . and partly that such an act by them done might be as firm as any patent, and in some respects more sure."[2] Nowhere is the compound of theological, communal, political, and economic dimensions of the federal tradition represented in such brief compass. This covenant, with twentieth-century spelling, reads as follows:

> In the name of God, Amen. We whose names are underwritten, the loyal subjects of our dread Sovereign Lord King James, by the Grace of God of Great Britain, France and Ireland King, Defender of the Faith, etc., Having undertaken, for the Glory of God and advancement of the Christian Faith and Honour of our

King and Country, a Voyage to plant the First Colony in the Northern Parts of Virginia, do by these present solemnly and mutually in the presence of God and one another, Covenant and Combine ourselves together into a Civil Body Politic, for our better ordering and preservation and furtherance of the ends aforesaid; and virtue hereof to enact, constitute and frame such just and equal Laws, Ordinances, Acts, Constitutions and Offices, from time to time, as shall be thought most meet and convenient for the general good of the Colony, unto which we promise all due submission and obedience. In witness whereof we have hereunder subscribed our names at Cape Cod, the 11th of November, in the year of the reign of our Sovereign Lord King James, of England, France and Ireland the eighteenth, and of Scotland the fifty-fourth, Anno Domini 1620.[3]

It would be difficult, perhaps impossible, to compose a statement that summarizes more completely and concisely the basic elements of the federal tradition as it emerges from Zurich and is developed in the Reformed communities of Europe. In order to understand the Mayflower Compact, it is necessary, first of all, to rid our minds of the glorification of the "Pilgrim Fathers" on which their social-climbing descendants in nineteenth-century New England based their self-serving histories of American society. This was a group of religious and social dissenters who had been forced to leave England and go to the Netherlands. The more tolerant climate there, however, did not permit the life they sought. So these refugees from Europe became the first "boat people" to immigrate into what was to become the United States. In Britain, they had been persecuted outsiders. In Holland, they were tolerated outsiders, excluded in large measure from cultural, political, and economic participation in Dutch society. Though neither in fear for their lives in the Netherlands nor desperately poor, they nevertheless set out on an uncertain, very perilous enterprise in the hope of establishing a society shaped by their own convictions, which were federal.

From their federal heritage, the Pilgrims had learned to be social realists. No one is ever outside a covenantal context, in some imaginary state of nature, but always exists symbiotically within a network of social compacts. These implicit agreements, however, need periodically to be made explicit and renewed. No time could be more necessary for renewal of the covenant than when a group has left a social context with a settled, operating government and is going into a situation in which social stability and government must be newly constructed if they are to be secure. The Mayflower Compact was not, therefore, a meaningless ritual but was a necessary federal action affirming the religious and communal basis on which specific governmental and social instrumentalities would be developed. It is not the words themselves that are primary but rather the action of commitment in the presence of God and one another that the words express.

The compact began by acknowledging the political reality of Great Britain and its king, James I, under the auspices of which the colony was being founded. The affirmation then moved to the common purpose of establishing the colony. The core of the document followed, in which, "solemnly and mutually in the presence of God and one of another," they "Covenant and Combine ourselves together into a Civil Body Politic, for our better ordering and preservation and furtherance of the ends aforesaid." The covenant included the commitment to set up whatever governmental instrumentalities are appropriate and the promise to give "all due submission and obedience" to these community decisions. Consent of the governed was considered crucial, yet, remembering the right and responsibility of the people to require adherence to the covenant on the part of the magistrates, it was due submission and obedience that was promised. The Mayflower Compact was a very firm yet conditional agreement that assumed a previous ordering of society to be continued, renewed, and improved. This religious-political covenant emerged from the federal tradition, fitted into it admirably, and established a clear pattern of federalism among the British colonies in the New World, a pattern that was to be replicated and extended.

The Puritans

The Puritan movement emerged as a Reformed and reforming impulse within the Church of England. It was not initially in any way separatist. Its purpose was to purify Anglicanism of its undesirable elements held over from Roman Catholicism. At first very successful among the laity, clergy, and bishops, Puritanism faced an increasingly strong high-church reaction in the late sixteenth century. Under James I, who had learned to hate Presbyterianism as James VI of Scotland, the high-church tendencies within the English church gained royal support, and, with the accession of Charles I, the Puritans came under increasing pressure to conform to the high-church convictions of the hierarchy or face persecution.

As well-to-do members of the growing middle class, the Puritans were not without financial resources and influential contacts at the court of the king. Plans were laid to secure a charter from the Crown for a trading company to operate in New England and to establish a colony there to which endangered Puritans in England could immigrate. A charter was indeed secured, and, beginning in 1628, numerous immigrants went to the New World to settle in the strong and well-financed Massachusetts Bay Colony.

John Winthrop (1588–1649), who served many terms as a magistrate, led a group that arrived in 1630 and voiced his federal views in the well-known address given aboard the *Arbella* before they went ashore: "Thus stands the cause between God and us: we are entered into covenant with Him for this work."[4] He elaborates his understanding in a speech to the General Court in 1645 that contains echoes of Althusius:

> It is yourselves who have called us to this office; and being called by you, we have our authority from God. . . . We account him a good servant who breaks not his covenant. The covenant between you and us is the oath you have taken of us, which is to this purpose, that we shall govern you and judge your causes by the rules of God's law and our own, according to our best skill. . . . There is a twofold liberty—natural (I mean as our nature is now corrupt), and civil or federal. The first is common to man, with beasts and other creatures. By this, man, as he stands in relation to man simply, hath liberty to do what he lists; it is a liberty to evil as well as good. This liberty is incompatible and inconsistent with authority. . . . The other kind of liberty I call civil or federal; it may also be termed moral, in reference to the covenant between God and man in the moral law, and the political covenants and constitutions amongst men themselves.[5]

The charter from the king, originally for a trading company governed internally by covenant and contract, became the basis for the government of the Massachusetts Bay Colony. The charter, as it became a frame for civil polity, was interpreted in a federal manner by the Puritan leaders of the colony. Indeed, the entire leadership of Massachusetts Bay in the early generation is profoundly federal in its theology, ethics, and political philosophy.

John Cotton (1584–1652), preacher, theologian, and civic leader, emphasized the federalist conviction that the sinfulness of humanity requires the limitation of power. In this regard he wrote:

> It is therefore most wholesome for magistrates and officers in church and commonwealth never to affect more liberty and

authority than will do them good, and the people good: for whatever transcendent power is given will certainly overrun those that give it and those that receive it. . . . It is necessary, therefore, that all power that is on earth be limited, church-power or other. If there be power given to speak great things, then look for great blasphemies, look for a licentious abuse of it. . . . It is therefore fit for every man to be studious of the bounds which the Lord hath set: and for the people, in whom fundamentally all power lies, to give as much power as God in His word gives to men.[6]

The government of the Massachusetts Bay Colony was not a democracy but rather a republic. In his "Letter to Lord Say and Seale" in 1636, Cotton makes it clear that the brand of federalism he espouses is not to be interpreted as democratic. "Democracy," he wrote, "I do not conceive that ever God did ordain as a fit government either for church or commonwealth." He affirms instead an order based on covenant "where a people choose their own governors; yet the government is not a democracy, if it be administered, not by the people, but by the governors."[7] This view may strike the twentieth-century reader as strange. Today a republic is seen as a kind of democracy. The fears of mob rule and disorder if government were controlled directly by the people were too great in the seventeenth century for many to favor what they called democracy. The gradual and careful change from a very high republican form of government in the first years of the Massachusetts Bay Colony toward greater democratization has taken place if one takes note of the evolution of political order in the British colonies prior to the American Revolution and in the United States afterward. The United States today, however, still has a republican form of government, not a democracy in the sense that Cotton rejected.

In its earliest days, the civil order in Massachusetts Bay tended strongly toward oligarchy. In 1630, however, when the magistrates attempted to turn themselves into a self-perpetuating body, the freemen of the colony demanded that the charter be followed and that the magistrates be selected by the vote of all the freemen for specified terms of office. To prevent the decisions of the magistrates from being too arbitrary, the freemen forced the adoption of a "Body of Liberties" in 1641, a move that in its purpose and its form resembles the Bill of Rights that was added to the U.S. Constitution in 1791.

At first in the Massachusetts Bay Colony, the basic law-making body was a meeting of all the freemen with the magistrates in what was called the General Court. As the increasing number of people made this form unwieldy, the General Court became a representative assembly with deputies elected from every town by the freemen. In 1642, the magistrates began meeting separately from the deputies at the General Court, thus turning the government of the colony into a bicameral system. The civil orders of the Hartford Colony, established under the leadership of Thomas Hooker (1586–1647), and of the New Haven Colony, with the guidance of John Davenport (1597–1670), resembled that of Massachusetts Bay. And all four, including Plymouth, represent the federal thought and practice that the Pilgrims and the Puritans brought with them.

Federalism in the Colonies:
New England to the Articles of Confederation

The influence of the federal tradition was felt beyond the bounds of New England and after the initial period of settlement. Rather than waning, federal thought and practice persisted and gathered strength during the colonial period.

Illustrations of this trend in the political patterns of New England are plentiful. The agreements by which towns were established—for example, Salem, 1629; Cambridge, 1632; Dorchester, 1633—were covenants. The Fundamental Orders of Connecticut in 1639, the New Haven Plantation Covenant in 1638 and Fundamental Articles in 1639, the Dover Combination (New Hampshire) in 1639, the Plantation Agreement at Providence in 1640, and the Massachusetts Body of Liberties in 1641 are further examples. In 1643 the New England Confederation was formed to unite the colonies of the northeast for purposes of defense against hostile Indian groups. Some Indian tribes joined with the colonies in this alliance, a move easy for them because the tribal and intertribal patterns among the Native Americans were also covenantal in form.

Covenant-like, or federal, agreements are also to be found throughout the colonies. The Act Establishing Assembly and Laws and the Acts for Swearing Allegiance and for People's Liberties in Maryland in 1638 were covenants as also were the Laws Regulating Church Government in Virginia in 1642, the Maryland Toleration Act of 1649, the Concession and Agreements of New Jersey in 1664, the Concession/Agreements of Proprietors of Carolina with Settlers in 1665, the Fundamentals of West New Jersey in 1676 and 1681, Penn's Charter of Liberties and Frame of Government for Pennsylvania in 1682, the Fundamental Constitutions for East New Jersey in 1683, and the Charter of Liberties and Privileges in New York in 1683. The continuing attempts to join the colonies together—for example, William Penn's Plan of Union in 1697 and Benjamin Franklin's in 1754—further illustrate the pervasiveness of federalism in the political thought and practice of the colonial period.

Donald Lutz, a political scientist, has accumulated an even more extensive list of covenant-like documents throughout the colonial era. He points out, however, that works dealing with the background to the Constitution usually fail to take this long procession of documents or even the state constitutions into account. He writes:

> If we were to pick up any book that proclaimed itself to be about American constitutional history, it would probably exhibit two traits characteristic of such books. First, it would focus almost entirely upon the national Constitution. Second, it would examine only what has happened since 1789. And discussion of where that Constitution comes from is (with a few notable exceptions) likely to be limited to a few remarks about the Magna Carta, the English Constitution, and probably the Declaration of Independence. This attitude toward the colonial portion of American political thought is so prevalent, that one writer recently remarked that, "For theoretical as well as practical purposes the origin of the American track can, therefore, be assumed to begin in 1776. The thinkers, issues, and events prior to 1776 have never really had a central impact on the conduct of American politics."[8]

Though ignored by most historians of the Constitution, there is a tradition of federalism that pervaded the entire colonial era, developed in distinctive ways apart from European thinkers, and formed the background of experience upon which the leaders of the Revolution and new nation relied as they shaped the institutions of what became the United States of America. When the Resolution for Independence was passed by the Continental Congress on June 7, 1776, it directed that a declaration be drawn up and that "a plan of confederation be prepared and transmitted to the respective Colonies for their consideration and approbation."[9] In continuation of the federal pattern, the Articles of Confederation for the United States of America were passed by Congress on November 15, 1777, were ratified by all the colonies except Maryland, and became effective on March 1, 1781. During the Revolution and the time when the government was carried out under the Continental Congress and the Articles of Confederation, the colonies that had been governed by charters from the Crown wrote constitutions for themselves, now that they had become states. These new frames of government built also on the experience of the past and followed the long tradition of federalism in the colonies, and thus illustrated, continued, and strengthened that tradition as the new nation emerged.

It is not surprising, therefore, to find William C. Morey, a political scientist, writing about the sources of the Federal Constitution:

> The origin of the forms of the federal government presents no great historical difficulty to one who has carefully studied the constitutional history of the early states and colonies. He finds that the central government of the United States, in its general structure, and its various branches, is scarcely more than a reproduction on a higher plane of the governmental forms existing in the previous states, and remotely in the early colonies.[10]

Varieties of Federalism in European Political Thought

The major sources of federalism in America were the federal theology, the federal political philosophy, and the federal practice in societal institutions brought by groups coming from Europe to establish colonies and developed in distinctive ways in the 180 years from Jamestown to Philadelphia. At the same time, federal thought continued to develop in Europe. Indeed, it can be found in some of the major political philosophers of the seventeenth and eighteenth centuries. These thinkers deserve mention in order to indicate the strength and variety of federalism and also because they undoubtedly had influence on the strong and distinctive form of federalism that was taking shape in the British colonies.

Hobbes

Born in Westport, near Malmesbury, and educated at Magdalen College, Oxford, in classical literature and theology, Thomas Hobbes (1588–1679) is one of England's foremost philosophers and must be regarded as a distinguished representative of the federal tradition, though he is more pessimistic about human nature and more royalist in politics than are Althusius, Rutherford, and most federalists of his time. His pessimism about existence is summed up in his most famous saying: "Human life is nasty, brutish, and short," that is, if action is directed by passions outside secure social compacts.

Hobbes's own life was, by contrast, comfortable, urbane, and long, because he prudently found ordered contexts in which to live.

At Oxford, Hobbes was trained in the Puritan covenantal tradition. He was acquainted with such outstanding contemporaries as Bacon, Descartes, Gassendi, and Galileo and was influenced by them. Yet the basic structure of his philosophy and theology remains federal, in his distinctive variation of this tradition. Nowhere is this clearer than in his political thought, the major statement of which appears in *Leviathan*, published in 1651.[11]

Leviathan is a treatise in theological politics or, in an older sense, political theology. Its political philosophy is profound because of its depth of insight into social and political process and also because of the theological depth of its insight into human nature, religion, and God. Over half the work deals directly with religion, and the entire discussion, from beginning to end, is founded on will and artifice within a covenantal understanding of God's relation to the world and human interaction within society.

The commonwealth or state, Hobbes explained in his introduction, was produced by the will and art of humans in imitation of that will and art by which God created the world. "Nature, the art whereby God hath made and governs the world," he wrote, "is by the *art* of man, as in many other things, so in this also imitated, that it can make an artificial animal." And the instrument of God's work and that of humans was federal. As Hobbes put it, "The *pacts* and *covenants*, by which the parts of this body politic were at first made, set together, and united, resemble that *fiat*, or the *let us make man*, pronounced by God in creation."[12] In order to describe this creation of humanity, Hobbes then proceeded, in the four major sections of the work, to consider: first, humans, whose will and art create the state in imitation of the covenantal creation of the world by God; second, how and by what covenants the state is made, and the just powers of the sovereign within the covenants; third, the Christian commonwealth; and fourth, the kingdom of darkness. As Hobbes elaborated his views, covenants, and the consent of the governed in covenant, provide the basis of government, with the rights of humans ceded to the sovereign through representation. Justice meant keeping the societal covenant, and, because Hobbes had a very pessimistic view of human nature, the covenantal promises must be reinforced by the power of the sovereign to make sure that the promises would be kept and the well-being of all remain secure.

Though God is sovereign of creation by power, God is sovereign of the people of God by covenant, that is, by their responsive consent. The opposition to the reign of God and of justice in society is named by Hobbes "the kingdom of darkness," which is, in line with his federal perspective, called "a confederacy of deceivers."

With regard to popular sovereignty, Hobbes does not fit easily into the framework of federal political philosophy that had prevailed since the days of Mornay and Althusius. Hobbes explicitly denied the right of resistance, even against a tyrant, for any reason, political or religious. With his affirmation of the sovereignty of the chief magistrate over matters both civil and religious, he echoed Bullinger, the founder of the Reformed federal tradition.

Locke

The notion of popular sovereignty was, however, powerful in itself. Mornay's *A Defense of Liberty Against Tyrants* clearly had something to do with the resilience of the ideal of popular sovereignty in England in the seventeenth century. Mornay's treatise had been published in an English translation in 1622, then reprinted in 1631 and 1648, the year before the execution of Charles I. Then it was reprinted twice more, in 1660, at the time of the Restoration, and in 1689, just after the Glorious Revolution. The core of Locke's argument on the federal nature of government and on tyranny can be found in Mornay's treatise, and Locke did own a copy of it.[13]

Born in Wrington, Somerset, John Locke (1632–1704) was reared in a Puritan household. His father fought on the side of parliament against Charles I. So Locke had already acquired a perspective within Puritan federalism prior to his education at Christ Church College, Oxford. After receiving his B.A. and master's degrees there, he remained to teach Latin, Greek, and moral philosophy. In 1661, Locke's father died, leaving him a small inheritance. The independence this gave him permitted Locke to broaden his education. He studied the new science and its methods with Robert Boyle and medicine with Thomas Sydenham. After travels on the Continent, where he became acquainted with the thought of Descartes, he began to apply himself seriously to philosophy, though it was quite late in life before he published his views and then tended to do it anonymously.

Because of his close association with the Earl of Shaftesbury, a leader of the parliamentary group opposing the policies of the Stuart kings, Locke was forced to take refuge in Holland in

1683. After the overthrow of James II in 1688 and the accession of William and Mary of Orange, Locke returned to England. In 1689, he published his *First Letter Concerning Toleration* and the *Essay Concerning Human Understanding*, on both of which he had worked for some time. In 1690 he published *Two Treatises of Government*, which also represent many years of labor. His reputation as a major political philosopher rests upon these works.[14]

The federal thought that appeared in his political philosophy is a milder, less pessimistic version of federalism than that to be found in Hobbes. The first of the *Two Treatises* was a critique of the notion of the divine right of kings held by Robert Filmer, a supporter of the Stuart monarchy. The second treatise, in which Locke sets forth his own political thought, opens with the proposal that humans originally were in a state of nature, in which they enjoyed perfect freedom within the bounds of the law of nature. The law of nature rests on the will of God. Because they are not perfect, humans in the state of nature fail to preserve peace and uphold the rights of others. It becomes necessary to form a civil government, accomplished when humans by consent enter into a social contract to create a political order. Within the political order, specific governmental arrangements are made and magistrates charged with ruling. If a ruler breaks his agreement with the people and becomes a tyrant, they may overthrow him. Sovereignty resides, as in Althusius, with the people in covenant and is exercised by a legislative body, made up of representatives of the people, an executive, and a judiciary, all of which are the agents of the people.

Hume

Born in Edinburgh and educated at the University of Edinburgh, David Hume (1711–1776) is the Scottish philosopher known better for having awakened Immanuel Kant from his dogmatic slumbers than for his own philosophical writings. The work that future generations of scholars have regarded as demonstrating his brilliance was completed when Hume was relatively young, and it was generally ignored in his lifetime. His applications for academic posts were turned down, and it was primarily as a writer of history that he was known by his contemporaries. He held various public appointments, was well known and well liked as a good conversationalist, and died of cancer at the age of sixty-five.[15]

Influenced by a broad spectrum of the philosophical and

scientific currents of the seventeenth and eighteenth centuries, Hume also shows that the Scottish federal tradition had significant impact upon him. His major tools of analysis in philosophy are the experimental method and a sharp skepticism. With these he is able to dismantle the metaphysical systems of rationalistic philosophers and the dogmatic systems of theologians. But, as Hume recognized, his methods could not touch the power of natural sentiments and convictions that shaped communal traditions and common sense. Indeed, the experimental method itself arises out of such a context, as also do the moral views and religious faith of ordinary society. The believing that shapes experience and affirms fact and morals derives from those implicit convictions held in community through covenantal relations embedded in tradition. Justice, therefore, is not, for Hume, a product of rational analysis but rather derives from tradition, is based on the invention or artifice of humans in particular social contexts, and serves the purposes of the community. The basis of the artifice for developing a particular notion of justice is not a conscious contract among people but is the deeper level of agreement that can better be called convention or covenant.

It is not surprising that Garry Wills finds far more from Hume than from Locke in the U.S. Constitution and the people who developed it.[16] Wills is aiming his criticism at such thinkers as Louis Hartz, who regards the political philosophy of John Locke as the "single key" needed for the interpretation of American politics. According to Hartz, Locke incarnates liberalism, and it is his philosophy that has permeated U.S. society from the Revolution until today. "Locke dominates American political thought," Hartz writes, "as no other thinker dominates the political thought of a nation. He is a massive national cliché."[17] Hartz presents no historical evidence from documents stating the views of the founders. Instead, he elaborates a hypothesis based apparently on intuited similarities and is even incorrect in reading his own liberalism back into Locke.

American scholars tend to study European thinkers. When they find elements in the American past that resemble something they have read in the work of a British or a German or a French writer, it seems natural to them to suppose that the American element is the result of influence from the European source. While those who shaped the social institutions of colonial America, carried out the Revolution, and produced the U.S. Constitution might have had some indirect or direct influence on them from European thinkers, these American leaders were primarily persons who relied on their immediate context, the tradition in which they were trained, and the experience accumulated on American soil. The American sources become especially apparent as one studies the development of the federal tradition in the political patterns and institutions throughout the colonial period.

Witherspoon and Madison

The development and strength of the federal tradition in the colonies is clear. As has already been shown, the origins of federal political philosophy and theology can be traced even farther back. The line of development extends back through the Reformed communities of Britain, the Netherlands, and Germany, back to Zurich and Heinrich Bullinger. From the historical evidence, the case is strong that Bullinger's 1534 treatise, *The Covenant,* can be regarded as the fountainhead of this federal stream in the modern world.

At the Federal Convention in Philadelphia in 1787, the practical men of affairs who were gathered to revise the Articles of Confederation had acquired the political experience on which they relied primarily for prudent insight and action from the distinctively American federal tradition as it had evolved over 180 years. They were not, for the most part, scholars or ideologues but rather pragmatic, cautious, and successful revolutionaries now wanting to shape a stable and enduring social order. Though they represented varied sectional, political, and economic interests, there was a general principle of agreement among them. "The delegates both from former habits and present reasons," as Carl Van Doren puts it, "preferred a federated republic to a consolidated nation."[18]

All were in somewhat different ways products of the colonial federal tradition. Two persons, however, deserve special attention because they demonstrate the strength of federalism in the period of the Revolution and Constitutional Convention. In them also can be seen its renewal and transformation in that time so that it was made directly applicable to the changed conditions confronting the infant republic as contrasted with the situation of the colonies under British rule. The first is John Witherspoon (1723–1794), president of the College of New Jersey, delegate to the Continental Congress, and a signer of the Declaration of Independence. The second is James Madison (1751–1836), a student of Witherspoon's at the College of New Jersey, delegate to the Constitutional Convention of 1787, and later the fourth president of the United States.

Witherspoon

"Cousin America has eloped with a Presbyterian parson," wrote Horace Walpole in 1775. The cousin was the British colonies and the Presbyterian parson was John Witherspoon.[19] Witherspoon was born into a preacher's family in Scotland. He entered the University of Edinburgh at age thirteen, graduated with an M.A. at age seventeen, and continued in study for four years in the Faculty of Divinity, completing his formal education in 1743. He served thereafter in pastorates in the Church of Scotland, was elected moderator of the Synods of Glasgow and Ayer in 1759, and received an honorary doctorate of divinity from the University of St. Andrews in 1764. While still in Scotland, he spoke widely and published often, his most popular work being *Ecclesiastical Characteristics, or the Arcana of Church Polity*, a tract published first anonymously in 1753 and reprinted five times over the next ten years.

In 1768, Witherspoon accepted an invitation to become president of the College of New Jersey, founded in 1746 by Presbyterians and later known as Princeton University. He served as its head until his death in 1794. From the time of his arrival, the new president began traveling extensively throughout the colonies and writing articles for various publications. At first his activities were designed to publicize the college and raise money to mend its shaky finances. Gradually, however, as the situation of the college improved, he joined the opposition to the establishment of an Anglican episcopate in the colonies and became an enthusiastic supporter of the emerging revolutionary cause.

Witherspoon was an articulate exponent of federal theology and federal political philosophy, which he had learned in Scotland. In terms that are familiar in the federal heritage from Bullinger forward, Witherspoon taught that "baptism is the seal of God's covenant. Our covenant God is most fully described as Father, Son, and Holy Ghost." In creation, God made a covenant of works with Adam, who is "the federal head and representative of the human race, as he was then the natural head." The consequences of Adam's actions, therefore, would be shared by the whole human race. The result of Adam's disobedience and fall was that all humans come into the world "in a state of impurity or moral defilement."[20]

Though fallen so that humans misplace their love, giving it to created things rather than to God, humans are not totally incompetent morally or incapable of any good. The power of reasoning is corrupted, but there remains "the power of natural conscience," permitting a limited amount of optimism about government if there are structures to mitigate human evil and maximize the potential for good. "Every good form of government," he wrote, "must be complex, so that one principle may check the other. . . . They must be so balanced, that when every one draw to his own interest or inclination, there may be an overpoise upon the whole. . . . There must be always some *nexus imperii*, something to make one part necessary to the others. . . . To produce this *nexus*, some of the great essential rights of rulers must be divided and distributed." With human action shaped and limited by societal covenants, Witherspoon affirmed, the federal polity represents the promise of republican government by "putting into motion all human powers, . . . promoting industry . . . happiness . . . and every latent quality, and improving the human mind. Liberty is the nurse of riches, literature, and heroism."[21]

Madison

Born and reared in Virginia, James Madison was a devout, churchgoing Anglican. From ages eleven to sixteen he attended a boarding school run by Donald Robertson, to whom Madison attributed "all that I have been in life" and from whom he received a classical education and a moderate Puritan federal perspective. After leaving Robertson's school, Madison was tutored by the Rev. Thomas Martin, rector of a church near Montpelier, where the Madison family lived. Martin had graduated from the College of New Jersey and, probably because of his influence, Madison and his father decided that he should go there rather than to William and Mary in Williamsburg, Virginia.

At the College of New Jersey, Madison went through the required curriculum, which included Hebrew and Greek, study of the Bible and classical literature, contemporary science, and theology and political philosophy with John Witherspoon, who had arrived the previous year from Scotland to become president of the college. From this learned and energetic advocate of federalism who was already becoming known as a leader of the movement calling for resistance to Britain, Madison had his knowledge of and commitment to the federal tradition deepened.

As a student, Madison seriously considered entering the Christian ministry. Partly because of health reasons but partly also because of the influence of Witherspoon on him, Madison decided to enter public life as an advocate of American independence from Britain and of effective governance in a federal republic. Madison even stayed an additional year at Princeton to continue his studies with Witherspoon.

Soft-spoken in public assemblies and self-effacing in political affairs, Madison nevertheless had remarkable influence on the development of the United States because of his careful scholarship and the persuasive power of his tightly organized arguments. In preparation for the Federal Convention at Philadelphia, Madison did exhaustive research on the federal tradition and on the history of confederacies and their problems from biblical and classical times to his own day.

It is in the *Federalist Papers*[22] that the breadth of his federal perspective and the incisiveness of his political insight are best illustrated. These papers, written by John Jay, Alexander Hamilton, and Madison and published in New York newspapers in a successful attempt to persuade that state to ratify the new Constitution, offer one of the great masterpieces of political philosophy. The authors argued persuasively for the particular form of federalism set forth in the document just completed by the Convention in Philadelphia and appealed, not so much to political theory, but rather to history and to the experience of American society. Madison's essays also testified to how much he had learned from Witherspoon.

Concerning human nature, Alexander Hamilton was very pessimistic. Writing in Federalist No. 6, he said that "men are ambitious, vindictive, and rapacious." Madison shared a certain amount of this pessimism but, like his Princeton teacher, mitigated this enough to see hope in federal political processes. "The history of almost all the great councils and consultations held among mankind for reconciling their discordant opinions, assuaging their mutual jealousies and adjusting their respective interests," he wrote in Federalist No. 37, "is a history of factions, contentions, and disappointments, and may be classed among the most dark and degrading pictures which display the infirmities and depravities of the human character." In Federalist No. 55, however, he wrote: "As there is a degree of depravity in mankind which requires a certain degree of circumspection and distrust, so there are other qualities in human nature which justify a certain portion of esteem and confidence. Republican government presupposes the existence of these qualities in a higher degree than any other form."

Madison assumed most of the elements that are distinctive in the federal tradition. One of these is the restlessness of the human heart that produces continuing change. Madison had absorbed this understanding. He declared, "In framing a system which we wish to last for ages, we should not lose sight of the changes which the ages will bring."[23] In Federalist No. 51, he brought together many of the federal themes and with muted optimism proclaims the promise of a covenantal perspective. He wrote:

> Justice is the end of government. It is the end of civil society. It ever has been and ever will be pursued until it be obtained, or until liberty be lost in its pursuit. . . . In the extended republic of the United States, and among the great variety of interests, parties, and sects which it embraces, a coalition of a majority of the whole society could seldom take place on any other principles than those of justice and the general good. . . . It is no less certain than it is important . . . that the larger the society, provided it lie within a practicable sphere, the more duly capable it will be of self-government. And happily for the *republican cause*, the practicable sphere may be carried to a very great extent by a judicious modification and mixture of the *federal principle*."

The more closely the Federal Constitution and its background are examined, the clearer it becomes that the men who wrote it were deeply involved with the long federal tradition and especially were experienced in the distinctive patterns of federalism developed in the colonial period, a federalism with a past stretching back to Bullinger, to Zurich, and to *The Covenant* as the fountainhead of federalism.

Part Two

DE TESTA

MENTO SEV FOEDERE
Dei unico & æterno
Heinrychi Bullin
geri breuis
EXPOSITIO.

IESVS

HIC est filius meus dilectus in quo
placata est anima mea, ipsum audite.

Matthæi 17.

TIGVRI, IN AEDIBVS CHRI
STOPH. FROSCH. MENSE
Septemb. An. M. D. XXXIIII.

A Brief Exposition
of the One
and Eternal Testament
or Covenant of God

by Heinrich Bullinger

JESUS
This is my beloved Son,
in whom my soul is reconciled.[1]
Hear him!
Matthew 17:5

Zurich: Christopher Froschauer,
September, 1534[2]

---

1. *"Hic est filius meus dilectus in quo placata est anima mea, ipsum audite."* Bullinger used this sentence, or a variation of it, on the title page or on the last page of all his books, always using *placatus,* or the German equivalent *versonenen,* rather than *placitus,* which would be the correct Latin translation of the Greek word *eudokesa,* used in Matt. 17:5 (see Matt. 3:17, where *eudokesa* is also used).

2. Almost two years prior to the first publication of Calvin's *Institutes* in 1536. Bullinger had finished the manuscript of this treatise in November 1533. It was written during a period when the Anabaptists seemed to him to be an especially dangerous threat. For a detailed analysis of the circumstances under which Bullinger wrote the treatise, see J. Wayne Baker, "Church, State, and Dissent: The Crisis of the Swiss Reformation, 1531–1536," *Church History* 57 (1988): 135–152.

A Brief Exposition of the One and Eternal Testament or Covenant of God

Heinrich Bullinger

Translated by Charles S. McCoy and J. Wayne Baker
With notes by J. Wayne Baker

This brief discourse sets forth the one and eternal testament or covenant of God, which both the prophets, inspired with the divine spirit, and the apostles, commissioned by the Son of God, explained by writing entire books. As I begin, I especially pray for your spirit, Christ Jesus, in order that, imbued with it, I may be able to discourse clearly, briefly, soberly, and according to the analogy of faith concerning a subject that is difficult but at the same time necessary and useful.

First, however, in order that greater clarity and more certainty may enter into the entire discussion it seems that a specific, definite meaning ought to be established for the word "testament," (2b) because its usage varies in Scripture.

The Meaning of Testament

The Hebrew term *berith*, which the Septuagint always translated into Greek as *diatheke* and the Latin writers rendered as *testamentum*, sometimes signifies the inheritance that results from a will (*testamentum*). The Greek verb *diatithemai* means "to make a will," and therefore the phrase *o diathekas ooio* means "I leave something to heirs in a will." And to the Latin writers "to make a testament" means "to make known one's final will." By the word *testamentum* they mean "a testimony (*testimonium*) of our will." The jurist Ulpianus[3] said that the lawful expression of our will was anything that one wants to be executed after one's

---

3. Domitius Ulpianus (d. A.D. 228) was a Roman jurist who made major contributions to Roman legal literature.

death. Gellius[4] and after him Lorenzo Valla[5], contesting the etymology of the jurists, (3a) deny that the word *testamentum* is a compound word composed from *contestatio mentis* ("the calling of the mind as a witness"). They assert, rather, that it is a simple word derived from "an invoking as witness" (*contestatione*), just as, likewise, "a small shrine" (*sacellum*) is not composed from "sacred" (*sacro*) and "small room" (*cella*) but is a diminutive form of "a sacred place" (*sacro*). Further, from *testor,* which means "I make a will," comes *testator,* "one who makes a will."[6] And it is with this meaning that Christ used the word in Matthew, ch. 26 [v.28], as did Paul in his letters to the Galatians, ch. 3 [15–18], and to the Hebrews, ch. 9 [15–17]. It is used extensively in this sense also among jurists. Second, the Greek phrase *diatithemai anti toi suntithemai* means "I make a pact" and "I make an agreement." Therefore, *diatheke* in the singular means "a pact," "an agreement," "a promise," that is, in Greek *epaggelia.* And among Latin writers, from *teste* (3b) comes the word *testor* which properly means "I give evidence" and "I affirm by oath." For this reason *testamentum* in Scripture is used several times for a "promise," not of any sort, but one confirmed by oath. Zechariah says in Luke [1:72, 73]: "In order that he might remember his sacred testament which he swore to our fathers that he would give us." And Peter says in Acts [3:25]: "You are sons of the prophets and of the testament which God swore to our fathers." Finally[7], *diatheke,* or *diathekai*

---

4. Aulus Gellius (b. ca. A.D. 130) was a Latin author whose major work, *Noctes Atticae,* or *The Attic Nights,* consisted of excerpts from authors of his day on a variety of topics, such as language, philosophy, law, and history.

5. Lorenzo Valla (ca. 1407–1457), an Italian Renaissance humanist, was a pioneer in textual criticism. It was Valla who exposed "The Donation of Constantine," the document on which the papacy based its claims to temporal supremacy, as a forgery. He was also quite important in setting the Renaissance standards of Latin literary style.

6. This entire discussion was lifted almost verbatim from Gellius's *Noctes Atticae* 7.12.1–6. See *The Attic Nights of Aulus Gellius,* with an English translation by John C. Rolfe, 3 vols., Loeb Classical Library (London, 1927), 2:123.

7. Bullinger published his own German translation of this treatise, also in 1534 (*Von dem einigen und ewigen Testament oder Pundt Gottes* [hereafter cited as *Von dem Testament*], which has been consulted to clarify Bullinger's meaning in the Latin version. Here it is clear from the German that Bullinger has presented three different meanings of *testamentum*: the first meaning had to do with a last will or the inheritance itself; the second meaning signified a promise confirmed with an oath; the third meaning was , covenant (*foedus*). He went on to state clearly that the third meaning—covenant—was the basic meaning of *testamentum* in this treatise. Although the Latin text uses only *rursus* and *item* to make the progression from point to point, leaving the possible impression that the second and third meanings could simply be shades of meaning, the German makes it clear that three different meanings are being discussed, using *item* and then *ze letst* (*Von dem Testament,* sigs. Aii(v) and Aiii).

in the plural, means "pact" and also "covenant" (*foedus*), to which the Hebrew word *berith* most closely corresponds. *Berith* is derived from *barah*, that is, "he made a pact" or "he entered into a covenant." Moses used it with this meaning in Genesis 15 and 17. We too shall use it in this way in the present treatise.

(4a) Latin grammarians think that *foedus* derives from the circumstance that in the making of a covenant (*foedus*) a pig was "horribly" (*foede*)[8], that is, cruelly, slain. Indeed, a covenant is properly made between enemies when ending a war. Though it puts forth proposals for harmony and fellowship, yet it is still entered into solemnly and with special ceremonies and conditions. For in the covenants of the ancients there were certain ceremonies, conditions, restrictions, or principles, or, if you prefer, main points. Under these conditions one may enter into a covenant for its duration. The chief negotiator who confirms[9] the covenant gives agreement with formalized words and ceremonies. Then, immediately, the records containing the account of the entire document are written, describing and transmitting the covenant in writing to posterity. In fact, in wills also, (4b) the arrangement is scarcely different, inasmuch as the heirs are first written down, then the inheritance is described, as well as those who are to be excluded from the inheritance. Everything is recorded and then signed and sealed so that no fraud may occur. However, as long as the death of the testator does not occur, the will does not take effect. But what is the purpose of this discussion? The point is that the very God who has graciously deigned to call this mystery of the unity and fellowship with the divine by a human expression has at the same time followed human custom, on account of the weakness of our nature, in making the covenant or instituting the testament. Thus, I shall be acting most appropriately if I proceed in this order, by the way of the conditions of the covenant, to discuss the one and eternal covenant of God.

---

8. *Foede* is an adverb derived from the adjective *foedus*—"foul" or "horrible." But the etymology and the play on words here are more complex than that. To make a covenant is *ferire foedus*, one meaning of *ferire* being "to kill." Thus the metonymy "to make a covenant" from "to kill a sow cruelly." See Karl Ernst Georges, *Ausführliches Lateinisch-Deutsches Handwörterbuch*, 12th ed. (Hannover, 1969), 1:2723.

9. The Latin term is *fetialis*. In the German edition, Bullinger used *pater patratus* (*Von dem Testament*, sig. Aiii). In either case, the reference is to the chief priest of a group of priests, who concluded and sanctified treaties and covenants (Georges, *Handwörterbuch*, 1:2742–2743; 2:1507).

(5a) The Record of the Covenant

The following words of Moses, which are set forth in this passage from Genesis, ch. 17 [1–14], testify to the fact that God entered into a covenant with us according to human custom: "Now when Abraham was ninety-nine years old, the Lord appeared to him and said to him: 'I am the almighty, all-sufficient God. Walk before me and be upright.[10] And I will make my covenant between me and you and between your seed after you in your generations an everlasting covenant, that I may be your God and the God of your seed after you. And I will give to you and to your seed after you all the land of Canaan as an everlasting possession, and I will be their God. And you on your part will keep my covenant, you and your seed in their generations. This is my covenant (5b) between me and you and your seed after you. Every male from among you will be circumcised. The male, however, whose flesh shall not have been circumcised on the foreskin, his soul will be blotted from his people, because he has made my pact void.' " These are the words of the covenant, not written down verbatim but brought together and united in a summary. If you examine these words carefully, you will see that God has acted according to human custom at every point. First, the passage explains who bound themselves together, namely, God and the descendants of Abraham. Second, the text states the conditions under which they bound themselves together, specifically that God wished to be the God of the descendants of Abraham and that the descendants of Abraham ought to walk uprightly before God. Third, it is explained that the covenant is made between them forever. And finally, the entire covenant is confirmed with a specific ceremony (6a) in blood. I should explain why there is no mention of legal records. Indeed, in place of such records are the words of Moses which we have already quoted, or, if you prefer more abundant words, the whole canonical Scripture. Thus nothing now remains except to speak specifically about each aspect of the covenant.

God's Covenant with the Descendants of Abraham

The ineffable mercy and divine grace of the eternal God are proven, first, in that God offers this covenant not in any way

---

10. It is quite clear in the German text that Bullinger uses *integer* in the moral sense: "*Schick dich vor mir zewandlen und biss ufrecter redlicher dingen/ trüw und ganggheylig an mir*" ("Prepare yourself to walk before me and do upright, honest things, true and holy to me"). (*Von dem Testament*, sigs. Aiii(v)–Aiiii.)

because of the merits of humans but rather out of the sheer goodness which is God's nature. I do not know whether humans are capable either of conceiving this mystery fully or conveying how praiseworthy it is. For what greater deed than this has ever been heard of in the world, that the eternal power and majesty, the immortal (6b) all-knowing God, the creator of the universe, in whom all things subsist, by whom all things exist, and through whom all things are preserved, joined himself in covenant with miserable mortals corrupted by sin. This indisputably is the origin of our religion and its primary point: we are saved solely through the goodness and mercy of God. Without doubt, this is what the prophet of God proclaimed to the whole world in a sacred song: "The Lord is holy and full of grace, slow to anger and great in mercy. He does not blame forever nor does he bear anger to eternity. He does not deal with us according to our sins, nor punish us according to our iniquities. As far as the heavens are high (7a) above the earth, so does God's steadfast mercy prevail toward those who fear him. As far as the east is from the west, so far does God remove our transgressions from us. As a father has mercy on his children, so does the Lord have mercy on those who fear him. For he knows how we are made, and that we are from the dust" [Psalm 103]. So whatever we are and whatever things have been created for our use and delight, we owe to the divine goodness and mercy. For God created all things for the benefit of humans. God has exhibited in many ways powerful demonstrations of his steadfast mercy toward humanity. Thus he raised up the faithless and fallen Adam immediately and ordered him to be of good hope (Genesis 3). And when the entire progeny and posterity of Adam deserved to be completely destroyed because of heinous crimes, (7b) God not only exercised justice when the flood engulfed the earth but also showed his steadfast mercy abundantly to Noah and his sons (Genesis 8). Why did he manifest the same mercy most clearly before the eyes of all mortals by making the everlasting covenant with Abraham and his posterity? So that I can now say the same of God and his goodness that Sallust[11] said of Carthage: "It is far better to be silent than to say little." But I prefer this saying above all others: "The same God who made covenant with Abraham and his

---

11. Gaius Sallustius Crispus (86 B.C.–ca. 34 B.C.) was a Roman historian. This quotation is from his work, *The Jugurthine War* 19.2. See Sallust, with an English translation by John C. Rolfe, Loeb Classical Library (Cambridge, Mass., 1947), p. 175.

descendants is the greatest possible God." Now we shall say a few words about the descendants of Abraham.

Who Are the Seed of Abraham?

And indeed one may easily get in trouble here unless one proceeds on the royal highway. For those people who consider only the conditions of the covenant and in fact disregard the grace and (8a) promise of God exclude infants from the covenant. It is true that children not only do not observe the terms of the covenant but also do not even understand these terms. But those who view only the sacrament, ceremony, or sign of the covenant count some in the covenant who are really excluded. But if you consider each one separately, one at a time, not only according to the conditions of the covenant but also in terms of the promise or the mercy of God, and the age and reason of a person, then you will realize that all those who believe from among the Jews and the Gentiles are the descendants of Abraham with whom the Lord made the covenant. In the meantime, however, their offspring, that is, their children, have by no means been excluded from the covenant. They are excluded, however, if having reached the age of reason they neglect the conditions of the covenant.

In the same way, we consider children (8b) of parents to be children and indeed heirs even though they, in their early years, do not know that they are either children or heirs of their parents. They are, however, disowned if, after they have reached the age of reason, they neglect the commands of their parents. In that case, the parent no longer calls them children and heirs but worthless profligates. They are mistaken who boast about their prerogatives as sons of the family by virtue of birth. For he who violates the laws of piety toward parents is no different from a slave; indeed, he is lower than a slave, because even by the law of nature itself he owes more to his parents. Truly this debate about the seed of Abraham has been settled for us by the prophets and the apostles, specifically that not everyone who is born of Abraham is the seed of Abraham, but only he who is a son of the promise, (9a) that is, who is faithful, whether Jew or Gentile. For the Jews have already neglected the basic conditions of the covenant, while at the same time they glorified themselves as the people of God, relying on circumcision and the fact that they were born from the parent Abraham. Indeed, this error is denied and attacked not only by Christ along with the apostles but also by the entire body of the prophets.

The People of the Old Testament, as a Spiritual People, with Spiritual Promises

We bring up this topic because of those who think that the first mention of the spiritual seed of Abraham was made in the New Testament. Compare Jeremiah, ch. 4, where the prophet examines the true circumcision, with chapter 2 in Paul's letter to the Romans; compare what Isaiah, Jeremiah, Ezekiel, and the other prophets wrote about the fidelity of the descendants of Abraham with what (9b) Christ said according to John, ch. 8, and with what Paul argued in his letters to the Romans and the Galatians. Then it will be quite clear that it was the same Spirit who spoke through the prophets and the apostles, both before and after the birth of Christ concerning the true seed of Abraham. Consequently, those things spoken in Scripture against the carnal seed and in favor of the spiritual seed were directed against those adults who have neglected the true piety of the soul while trusting in their birth and circumcision, or, if you prefer, trusting in the flesh and in the ceremony of initiation and taking pride in external things. Nevertheless, these passages of Scripture do not exclude children, born to faithful parents, who belong to God because of the grace and the call of the One who promises.

Children of the Faithful as the Seed of Abraham

For in this passage God has promised through grace and said, "I will be your God and the God of your seed (10a) after you." And even more clearly, "This is my covenant between you and me and your seed after you: Every male among you shall be circumcised." Again, lest anyone think this saying applies only to people of the Old Testament but not also to those of the New Testament, let him listen to Paul speaking in Galatians: "Those who are Christ's are the offspring of Abraham" (Gal. 3:29). Again, "Those who are heirs are the descendants of Abraham." Yet again, "Those who are holy are the seed of Abraham." If you connect these statements—they are children of Christ, they are heirs, they are holy—it follows automatically that the children are the seed of Abraham and they are in the covenant. Here the words of Christ are pertinent: "Let the little children come to me, for of such is the kingdom of heaven" (Luke 18:16). Also this passage from Paul: "For the unbelieving spouse is made holy through marriage to a faithful one. Otherwise, your children (10b) would be unclean, but they are now holy" (1 Cor. 7:14). Undoubtedly this happens through the grace and mercy of the Lord. But here some object: While the parent is unfaithful, a child born of him is excluded from the covenant. And they call "unfaithful" the one who profanes the name of the Lord with an impure life who otherwise confesses it with his mouth. But these who make such an objection do not consider the fact that the parent is once for all inscribed among the people of God and that the guilt of the parent does not spread to the children. The Lord has made this clear in the 18th chapter of Ezekiel. The sons of Israel were circumcised and called the people of God even though they had been born of evil parents, those whom the Lord struck down in the desert because of impious complaining. For God said, "Your sons and little ones who today (11a) are ignorant of the difference between good and evil will enter the land; I will give it to them, and they shall possess it" (Deut. 1:39). In like manner, the apostle clearly demonstrates in 1 Corinthians, ch. 7, how the Lord is gracious toward those children who are born of only one parent who confesses the name of the Lord. Now is it probable that the most merciful God acted less favorably and more harshly toward our children after he sent the Savior than he had acted toward those children whom he had chosen as his possession before Christ had been sent? No! Since it has been established sufficiently that their children, even those who have been born of evil parents, were circumcised and inscribed among the people of God, we have no doubts at all about the children of Christians, and we recommend that these children of the faithful be freely received into the church by baptism. (11b) I will say more about these things elsewhere. Concerning those things which have been explained up to this point, I think it is clear who are the seed of Abraham and that the inheritance is owed to this very seed.

The Conditions of the Covenant

Now we come to the conditions of the covenant. Those who are connected by covenants are joined together by certain regulations, so that each of the parties might know its duty, namely, what responsibilities the primary party might have toward the other, and what in return the primary party might expect from the other.

The Promises of God and His Offer of Himself in Covenant

Therefore God, who holds the primacy in this covenant, first expresses and sets forth the divine nature, as much as he wishes to show himself to us. Then God further explains what he demands from us in return, and what is fitting for us to do. For that reason with solemn words and with a great authority God thus declares: "I am (12a) the abundantly all-sufficient God, the horn of plenty." That is to say, he alone is that power and that good which suffices for humans. He who is in want of nothing supplies everything for everyone. Eternally he lives, moves, and acts from the divine energy itself. For this signifies at once everything that the Hebrew word *Shaddai* comprehends. By this name, the Lord wonderfully, felicitously, and concisely sets forth his unity, his omnipotence, and all his moral excellence and goodness. But since too great a brevity might generally lead to obscurity, God soon adds an explanation: "I will establish my covenant between me and you and your seed after you in order that I may be your God and the God of your seed after you." For it is not sufficient to have believed that God exists or even that he is all-sufficient unless you further (12b) believe that the same omnipotent God, the creator of all things, is your God, indeed the rewarder of all who seek him (Hebrews 11). Now in order that he might clearly show what it means to be the all-sufficient God, the God of the faithful and the rewarder of those who fear him, God adds as vivid examples for the covenanted people: "I will give to you and to your seed after you all the land of Canaan as an everlasting possession, and I will be their God" [Genesis 17:8].

The Promises to the Ancients
Not Entirely Carnal

Although these things promised about the land of Canaan were fulfilled physically (for the Lord also demonstrates his goodness in matters relating to the necessities of this life), they are nevertheless set forth with many terms about the eternal inheritance, especially life in heaven. Paul makes this point clearly with these words that he writes to the Hebrews, ch. 11 [13–16]: (13a) "Abraham, Isaac, and Jacob died in faith, at a time when they had not received the promises but had seen them from a distance and believed them, and had embraced them; and they confessed that they were strangers and foreigners in the land. For those who said these things declared that they sought a homeland. Yet if they had in mind that land whence they had come, they had the opportunity of returning. But now they expect a better land, that is, a heavenly one." The Lord spoke in like manner about the land of Canaan, but in doing so he also included other greater spiritual gifts and benefits. Furthermore, God wished to reveal to them what his nature is, or how his statement "I will be your God" should be understood. The other promises also serve as an explanation of this: "I will bless you and (13b) I will magnify your name and you will be blessed. I will bless those who bless you and I will curse those who curse you; and in you all the families of the earth will be blessed" [Gen. 12:2–3]. Again, "Fear not, Abraham, I will be your shield and your exceedingly great reward" [Gen. 5:1]. Once more, "I will multiply you as the stars of heaven and I will make you the father of many peoples" (Gen. 15 [5]).

From all these promises we are able to gain a full understanding that this God is the highest good, that he is our God, that he is all-sufficient, that he has made a covenant with us, and that the promises and conditions offered in that covenant are not only material but also spiritual. Most important, as explained to the Galatians [3:16] by the apostle, Abraham was promised the Lord Jesus, in whom is all fullness, righteousness, sanctification, (14a) life, redemption, and salvation (1 Cor. 1 [30]), of whose fullness we have all received, grace for grace (John 1 [16]), because it pleased the Father that all fullness dwell in him, and through his blood on the cross he has made peace with everything that is in heaven and on earth (Col. 1 [19–20]). And this same Jesus is the inheritance itself which has been bequeathed to those who trust in the one and eternal covenant of God, the summary of which (if anyone seeks a recapitulation) is this: The God of heaven, that highest and eternal power and majesty, through whom all things exist, in whom all things consist and are moved, wishes to be the God of Abraham and of his descendants. That is, God offers himself for their benefit, seeing that he is sufficient for all those things necessary for humans, so that now he might promise to them power and every kind of strength. Namely, (14b) God will be their protector, confederate, and savior, who is going to strengthen the otherwise weak human race in spirit and in flesh, and who through Christ the Lord is going to liberate the human race from sin and from eternal death and give eternal life. These things have to do with the office and participation of God in this covenant, the God who appeared to us under the cover of the land of Canaan and the blessed seed as the horn of plenty and all the treasures of heaven, and invited the entire human race to enjoy these blessings (Isaiah 55). Now let us listen to what God in return demands and expects from us.

The Duties of Humans and What They Owe to God

God says, "You will keep my covenant, you and your descendants in their generations. Walk before me and be upright." These, I say, are our duties; these things must be observed by us. And God says, "You (15a) will keep my covenant," that is, "You will trust me alone for all your needs in every situation and you will be faithful with all your heart to me alone." For thus also Moses explained in Deuteronomy 13 [4], saying, "Follow the Lord your God; fear him, keep his commandments, and listen to his voice! Serve him and cleave to him." What follows next in the actual words of the covenant? "Walk before me." It can be said that nothing is more brief, nothing more evident than these words—except that the phrase "to walk" according to Hebrew usage is the same as "to live," which we express idiomatically, "Prepare yourself to walk and to live uprightly."[12] And God adds, "before me," which means "according to my will and pleasure." Therefore the meaning is, (15b) "Arrange your life in every respect according to my will." Then, with these rather clear words, "and be upright!" God further explains what his will is and how we can walk before him. For firmness and sincerity of faith, along with innocence and purity of life, is that integrity and straight way by which the saints walk before God. Thus Moses in Deuteronomy 10 [12] also says, "And now, Israel, what does your Lord ask of you, except that you fear the Lord your God and walk in his ways, love him and serve the Lord God with your whole heart and with your whole soul?" And Micah 6 [8], "I will show you, O man, what is good and what the Lord requires of you: namely, to use good judgment and to love mercy and to walk carefully before your God." (16a) But what is central among these many things? It is our duty to adhere firmly by faith to the one God, inasmuch as he is the one and only author of all good things, and to walk in innocence of life for his pleasure. For anyone who has neglected these things and has sought false gods, who has lived shamefully or impiously, and who has worshiped God more with ceremonies or external things than with true holiness of life, will be excluded, disinherited, and rejected from the covenant.

---

12. *"Schickt dich wohl und raecht zewandlen und zelaebenn."* This is the only German sentence in the Latin edition. In the German edition, Bullinger wrote: *"Schick dich vor mir zewandlen. Das ist also vil geredt: flyss dich wohl und recht vor mir zelaeben"* (*Von dem Testament*, sig. Biii).

The Covenant—The Subject of All Scripture

The Covenant as a Target at Which All Scripture Aims

The entire sum of piety consists in these very brief main points of the covenant. Indeed, it is evident that nothing else was handed down to the saints of all ages, throughout the entire Scripture, other than what is included in these main points of the covenant, although each point is set forth more profusely and (16b) more clearly in the succession of times. For whatever things have been said in the Holy Scripture about the unity, power, majesty, goodness, and glory of God are included in this one expression of the covenant: "I am the all-sufficient Lord." Whatever promises have been written about bodily blessings, glory, the kingdom, victories, labors, and the basic needs of life, are included in this one expression of the covenant: "I will give to you and to your descendants the land of Canaan; I will be their God." In the same way, those things which have been handed down afterward at various times about Christ the Lord, both in figure and in truth, whatever has been said about his justice, about the sanctification and redemption of the faithful, about the sacrifice, the priesthood, and the satisfaction of Christ, about the kingdom and eternal life, and, further, about the calling of all peoples, (17a) about spiritual blessings, about the abrogation of the law, about the glory of the church gathered from Gentiles and Jews, are foretold in this single promise: "And all the nations will be blessed in you and you will be the father of many peoples; wherefore from now on your name is not Abram, but you will be called Abraham." Again, those things which have been said about faith in God, about the vanity of idols, about worshiping the one God, about the calling upon and the reverence of the one God, and also about true justice, about judgment, and about cultivating equity and charity—all of these things that have been transmitted through various laws, through the many discourses of the prophets, through the epistles of the apostles, and finally through the Gospel narratives, have been summed up in these few words: "You, however, shall keep my covenant, you shall walk before me, and you shall be complete or upright."(17b)

A Collation of the Entire Scripture Around the Main Points of the Covenant

Compare, if you will, the law, the prophets, and the very epistles of the apostles with these main points of the covenant, and you will discover that all of them return to this center as if to a target. For the law (as we shall speak about this first) truly teaches, with the Lord himself as a witness, partly the love of God and partly the love of the neighbor. This is precisely what is taught by the main points of the covenant. In fact, the Decalogue itself seems to be almost a paraphrase of the conditions of the covenant. For what is said in the brief phrase, "I am the all-sufficient Lord," is more fully explained by the Decalogue in approximately the same way: "I am the Lord your God who led you out of the land of Egypt." Again, what is proclaimed very concisely in the words of the covenant, "You will keep my covenant, you will walk before me, and you will be (18a) upright," is explained this way in the Decalogue by means of a specific list: "You shall not have other gods before me. You shall not make images for yourself. You shall not use the name of the Lord in vain. You shall keep the Sabbath holy. You shall honor your parents. You shall not kill. You shall not commit adultery," and whatever other commands of this sort there are that describe and establish true integrity.

We shall speak about ceremonies a little later, when we discuss the relationship of the Old and New Testaments.

Civil or Judicial Laws

The judicial or civil laws provide rules for the maintenance of peace and public tranquillity, for punishing the guilty, for waging war and repelling enemies, for the defense of liberty, of the oppressed, of widows, of orphans, and of the fatherland, and for the making of laws of justice and equity (18b) relating to the purchase, the loan, possessions, inheritance, and other legal subjects of this sort. Are not these things also included in that very condition of the covenant which prescribes integrity and commands that we walk in the presence of God? Now if anyone thinks that this opinion of ours is not valid or clear enough, let him consider the very deeds of Abraham, whom the apostle calls the father of all believers (Rom. 4 [11]). Abraham certainly endured faithfully within the covenant of God and walked uprightly before him. Insofar as judicial, civil, or external affairs are concerned, Abraham conformed to certain principles in punishing crimes, in making covenants, in declaring war, in preserving possessions and public peace—and these principles are nothing else than what purity of the soul, sincerity of faith, and love (19a) of virtue and the neighbor dictated. Indeed, much later, Moses, speaking for God, taught the Jewish people to observe the same principles (insofar as it pertains to the same substance and sum of the matter). For these are also the obligations of piety, or necessities for the holiest churches, so necessary that without them they could not properly exist, and they have never existed apart from them without danger. In connection with that, according to the word of the Lord (Matthew 13), there will always be tares in the field of the Lord, nor will it ever be without them. For the Lord did not wish the tares to be uprooted because their uprooting would ruin the wheat, that is, the righteous and the holy church. So Jesus said, "Allow both to grow, lest while you gather together the tares you at the same time also uproot the wheat with them." But who doubts that those same (19b) tares ought to be cut off with the scythe of justice, when their excessive and untimely strength and quantity tends toward the subversion of the church? Furthermore, the saints consist not only of spirit but also of flesh. As long as they live on this earth they do not entirely lay aside the human shape and totally turn into spirit. But also their laws are made to order external dealings among people in their social life. For these reasons, they need magistrates and the works of the civil law covering many subjects. What is more strange than the insanity that drives those who exclude[13] the magistrate from the church of God, as if there were no need of his functions, or who consider his functions to be of the sort that cannot or ought not to be numbered among the holy and spiritual works of the people of God? (20a) Nevertheless, those deeds of Abraham which are truly judicial are praised by the Holy Spirit of God as among the first and the most excellent works. Therefore that same Abraham, inasmuch as he was named the father of all believers by the apostle and called a friend of God prior to the law, possesses a foremost place in the true church of Christians; he nevertheless exercised judicial powers. Now we turn from the law to the prophets.

The Prophets

The prophets write partly history and partly discourses, which some call declamations and others sermons or homilies. In these histories they provide examples, indeed, nothing else but examples, of this covenant, just as Moses does in his

---

13. This is the closest Bullinger came to actually naming the Anabaptists in the entire treatise. For a succinct expression of the early Anabaptist attitude toward government, see the Schleitheim Confession of 1527, especially article 6 (John H. Yoder, trans. and ed., *The Legacy of Michael Sattler* [Scottdale, Pa.: Herald Press, 1973], pp. 39–40).

historical narrative, where one can see how God stood firm in his covenant, how he was the God of the seed of Abraham, (20b) that is, their all-sufficient defender, their salvation and their greatest happiness. One can also see how he led them into the land of Canaan where he made them into a most powerful kingdom, how he destroyed the enemies of the seed of Abraham by his powerful hand and mercifully protected his own people. Finally, one can see how the saints walked before him uprightly, that is, how they adhered to the one God through true faith and worshiped him in holiness of life, and furthermore, how some of them neglected this covenant and were punished for their impiety. Therefore the prophetic histories are like living paradigms of this covenant.

In their discourses the prophets also deal with nothing else but those same terms of the covenant, teaching what the nature of God is; how good he is; how just, powerful, (21a) truthful, kind, and merciful he is; how he must be served in truth, faith, righteousness, and love. Furthermore, they severely condemn crimes, especially the forsaking of the covenant, idolatry, desertion, and faithlessness, as well as murder, the oppression of the poor, usury, injustice, rape, extravagance, adultery, and other shameful crimes. They also urge repentance, they promise the rewards and the benefits of God, and they threaten plagues and the fearful punishments of God. Finally, how very clearly do they speak about the seed of Abraham, about Christ and his blessing, about the kingdom and its whole mystery, and about the calling of the Gentiles and the glory of the church. Indeed, at times they seem to have woven together not only prophecy but also a history of past events. (21b)

Christ, the Seal and Living Confirmation of the Covenant

What am I to say about Christ the Lord, who, not only in every teaching but also in his most astounding incarnation, explained and confirmed in a marvelous and living way that eternal covenant of God made with the human race? For when the true God assumed true humanity, then he no longer acted with words or arguments, but by that very event he bore witness to the greatest mystery in the entire world, namely, that God admitted humans into the covenant and into partnership, indeed that he bound them to himself with an indissoluble bond by the highest miracle of love, and that he is our God. Thence, truly we also believe the name given to Christ in Isaiah [7:14], when he is called "Emmanuel," which is to say, "God with us." Thence the Gospel writers (22a) recount those outstanding and

innumerable miracles and benefits of Christ, giving many examples. For in these ways Christ declared that he is the beneficent God, and what is more, the cornucopia, father and *Shaddai*
of the human race. The death and resurrection of Christ are
the most certain testimonies of divine mercy, justice, and life
restored, with which God has revealed himself, poured out his
entire self for us, blessing us and receiving us who have been
cleansed by him into partnership and into the eternal kingdom.
John the Evangelist said all of these things with a few, but
heavenly, words: "In the beginning was the Word, and the
Word was made flesh and dwelt among us. And we saw his
glory, the glory which was fitting for the only-begotten (22b)
from the Father, full of grace and truth. Of his fullness we have
all received, grace for grace. For the law was given through
Moses, but grace and truth appeared through Jesus Christ"
(John 1 [1, 14, 16–17]). Hear that greatest mystery: God was
made human, that is, was totally made one of us and has dwelt
among us. Hear that his power and glory have brought light
into the world, and for no other reason except to draw us by the
most beautiful benefits into his love, he who is our fullness, the
God *Shaddai*. For as Paul says, "In Christ dwells all the fullness
of the Godhead bodily, and you are completed and perfected in
him" (Col. 2 [9–10]). In this way, therefore, the Lord Jesus
confirmed and unfolded the first part of the covenant, by this
very fact (23a) pointing out that God is the God *Shaddai*, the
blessing and the eternal happiness of the seed of Abraham. The
other part of the covenant, as we have said, explains what God
in turn demands from us and what sort of people we should be,
which the Lord no less diligently and clearly has placed before
our eyes in Christ. He prescribed in the conditions of the
covenant: "Walk before me and be upright." Therefore, when
Christ the Lord came into this world, and entered into that path
of God, he left us a living example which we might follow. For
in the life of Christ, which the Gospels have described rather
diligently as in a mirror so to speak, we see what we ought to
follow or avoid, what pleases or what displeases God. Those
(23b) sayings of the Lord found in John's Gospel are pertinent
here: "I am the light of the world; he who follows me does not
walk in darkness, but has the light of life" (John 8 [12]). Or, "I
have given you an example, that just as I have done, so also you
should do" (John 13 [15]). That text in John's first epistle also
pertains to this: "He who says that he abides in Christ ought
himself to walk as that one walked" (1 John 2 [6]). These things
concern the life and living example of Christ.

Now there is no reason for me to treat what pertains to his

teaching at any length. For who does not know that he taught partly faith in God and partly love of the neighbor? The former explains the first aim of the covenant, the latter the second. For faith believes that God is the highest good, that he is righteous and beneficent toward humanity. And love (24a) is the fountainhead of innocence and uprightness of life.

The Apostles

We come to the apostles of Christ, the heralds of the Lord, who also are in agreement on this matter. They teach what the nature of God is, that he alone is good, righteous, saving, and *Shaddai*, that he has given to us the promised blessed seed of Abraham, and that in this one person there is salvation, benediction, life, and redemption. Furthermore, they teach who the heirs of this testament are, who the posterity of Abraham is, so that they are seen to have undertaken a most purposeful exposition of this covenant. Why does the apostle Paul declare more than once that he invents no new doctrine but teaches the whole of Christianity on the authority of the Old Testament? In the first chapter of Romans [vs. 1–2] he says that he was made an apostle (24b) and set apart for the preaching of God's gospel which God had promised beforehand through his prophets in the sacred Scripture. Furthermore, pleading his case before King Agrippa and Festus, the ruler of the Jews, Paul openly testified that he had taught nothing other than what the prophets had predicted would come to pass (Acts 26 [22]). Therefore, since the apostles recognize the prophets as teachers and masters of the true faith, and since it is absolutely certain that the prophets were interpreters of that single eternal covenant, who does not see that everything in sacred Scripture is directed to that testament or covenant as to a most certain target?

The Unity of the Covenant

The third point now follows from the above facts: the testament or covenant is both one and everlasting. For in plain words the Lord himself says among the other statements about his covenant: (25a) "I will make my covenant between me and you, and between your seed after you in their generations as an everlasting covenant, so that I may be your God and the God of your seed after you." In all that we have said up to this point, we have established nothing about true religion in relation to posterity that the ancestors had not already heard, certainly insofar as it pertains to the substance of the matter. Abraham was clearly justified by faith alone, without ceremonies, prior to circumcision and the law (Rom. 4 [1–13]). He saw the day of the Lord Jesus and rejoiced (John 8 [56]). Furthermore, he hoped for an everlasting fatherland, holding this earthly land in contempt, and thus searched for an eternal land, not merely a carnal or earthly one (Hebrews 11 [8–10]). Moreover, the apostles of Christ, indeed Christ the Lord himself, told us why Abraham must be imitated in faith and innocence (Luke 19 [9]). (25b) There can be no sameness or equality among things that are contrary by nature. If, therefore, the faith and innocence of Abraham had not been the true Christian faith and piety, then the Lord would have falsely proposed that he should be imitated by Christians (Isa. 51 [1–2]; John 8 [39–40]). There is therefore one covenant and one church of all the saints before and after Christ, one way to heaven, and one unchanging religion of all the saints (Psalms 14 and 23). And, indeed, I would offer several testimonies about this matter if the very point which we have treated up to now were not convincing to the doubter with its clarity and simplicity. But if anyone is more influenced by the force of testimonies, let him listen to the Lord himself speaking in Matthew: "A multitude will come from the east and from the west and will sit (26a) with Abraham, Isaac, and Jacob, while children of the kingdom will truly be cast forth into the outer darkness where there will be weeping and gnashing of teeth" (Matt. 8 [11–12]). Also in the Gospel of John [10:16], Jesus speaks more clearly about the gathering together of the church of the Gentiles: "And I have other sheep which are not of this fold, and it also behooves me to draw them in, and they will hear my voice and there will be one flock and one shepherd." In addition to this, several very clear parables in the Gospels are pertinent, especially the one about the wedding feast and those which deal with the vineyard (Matt. 20 [10–16]; 21 [33–41]; 22 [1–14]). In these parables the guests and the laborers are changed, but the wedding feast and the vineyard always remain the same. Not dissimilar to these is the parable of the apostle about the olive tree and the branches (Rom. 11 [17–24]). For the same olive tree always remains, the same tree, but (26b) the shoots of a wild olive tree are grafted in with the natural branches that have been broken off. Also, with eloquent words to the Corinthians, Paul says, "I do not wish you to be ignorant, brethren, that all of our fathers ate of the same spiritual food and all drank the same spiritual drink. For they drank of the spiritual rock which accompanied them. But the rock was Christ" (1 Cor. 10 [1–4]). But if our opinion and Paul's opinion from these texts seem to anyone to be a new interpretation, he should know that Doctor Aurelius Augustine drew the same conclusion as we did from this very text of Paul to the Corinthians. Augustine's words in his *Commentary On the Gospel of John*[14] support this interpretation: "The just ones who preceded the advent of our Lord Jesus who humbly came in the flesh believed in him who was to come in the same way that we believe (27a) in him who came. The times are different, but not the faith. Although the times did indeed differ, we see that those of both times entered through the one doorway of faith, that is, through Christ. We believe that our Lord Jesus Christ was born of a virgin, that he came in the flesh, that he suffered, rose, and ascended. Now we believe that *all of this*[15] already has been fulfilled, just as you heard the words in the past tense. Those fathers who believed that he would be born of a virgin, that he would suffer, would rise, and would ascend into heaven are in the fellowship of this faith with us. For the apostle made these things clear when he said, 'We have the same spirit of faith, just as it is written, "I believed and for that reason I have spoken, and we also believe and for that reason we speak." ' The prophet (27b) said: 'I believed and for that reason I have spoken' [Ps. 116:10]. The apostle says: 'We believe and for that reason we speak.' In order that you might know, however, that *there is one faith*, listen to him saying, 'Having the same spirit of faith, we believe.' And so in another place he says, 'I do not wish you to be ignorant, brothers,' " and what follows, for this text of Paul in 1 Corinthians 10 is familiar. Furthermore, Augustine, writing elsewhere[16] and speaking of the church, says, "The

---

14. *In Ioannis evangelium tractatus CXXIV* 45.9, in J. P. Migne, ed., *Patrologiae cursus completus, Series Latina* (Paris, 1844–1864), 35:1722–1723 (hereafter cited as *PL*). Philip Schaff, ed., *A Select Library of Nicene and Post-Nicene Fathers of the Christian Church, First Series* (New York, 1886–1889), 7:252 (hereafter cited as *PNF*).

15. The emphasis is Bullinger's.

16. *De baptismo contra Donatistas,* 1.16. 25 (*PL* 43:123; *PNF* 4:422). Donatism, a schismatic movement in the church in North Africa, began in the early fourth century. The dispute centered on whether *traditores*, those who had given their copies of the Scripture to the authorities during the Diocletian persecution, were eligible for priestly office. The Donatists argued that ordination, baptism, and other sacerdotal activities were not valid when performed by a *traditor*.

In A.D. 411, Augustine arranged a conference between the Donatists and the orthodox Catholics. Of those who attended, 286 were Catholic bishops and 279 Donatist bishops. The imperial commissioner declared Augustine and the Catholics the winners of the three-day disputation. The Donatists were ordered to conform under severe penalties, including death. Most of Augustine's writings against the Donatists came prior to A.D. 412, including *De baptismo*, which he wrote about A.D. 400.

same church that gave birth to Abel, Enoch, Noah, and Abraham also at a later time gave birth to Moses and the prophets before the coming of the Lord; and that very same church gave birth to our apostles and martyrs and all good Christians. For it gave birth to everyone who appeared, born at different times but joined together in the fellowship of one people; (28a) and the citizens of the same city have experienced the hardships of this pilgrimage, just as some are now experiencing them, and others will experience them until the end of the world." From all of this I think it is truly evident that there is only one church and one covenant, the same for the patriarchs and for us.

The Source of the Terms "Old" and "New" Covenant

Many arguments are found in Scripture that at first glance seem clearly to distinguish between two covenants, two peoples and two spirits, such as that which we read in Jeremiah 31 [31–32]: "Behold the days will come, says the Lord, when I will make a new covenant with the house of Israel and Judah, not according to the covenant I made with their fathers," etc. And again in Ezekiel 36 [26], "I will give you a new heart, and I will put a new spirit (28b) in your midst." Again in Galatians 4 [24], "These are the two covenants." Now I will explain from whence these terms were born and how they should be understood. To begin with, it is certain that the nomenclature of the old and new covenant, spirit, and people did not arise from the very essence of the covenant but from certain foreign and unessential things because the diversity of the times recommended that now this, now that be added according to the contrariety of the Jewish people. These additions did not exist as perpetual and particularly necessary things for salvation, but they arose as changeable things according to the time, the persons, and the circumstances. The covenant itself could easily continue without them.

Ceremonies

Indeed, the ceremonies are of this sort, as well as the Aaronic priesthood itself, the law prescribing the manner of sacrificing, purifying, (29a) and slaying, and even the choice of foods, what type of tabernacle had to be constructed, and innumerable other things of this sort. For the holy patriarchs were without such things—Enoch, Noah, Abraham, Isaac, Jacob, Joseph—

but they were nevertheless pleasing to God at a great cost through faith, and they attained salvation without such things. Wherefore Paul speaking to the Galatians, ch. 3 [16–17], says, "The promises were spoken to Abraham and to his seed. It does not say 'to his seeds' as of many, but only of one, 'And to your seed,' which is Christ. Moreover, I say, the law which originated 430 years later does not make void this covenant established earlier by God in Christ, so that it would abrogate the promise." Hence the patriarchs were saved by the blessing of the covenant, not of the law or of the ceremonies. (29b) For just as Abraham believed in him who had said, "In you all the nations of the earth will be blessed" (Gen. 22 [18]), so the fathers of Abraham preceding him in time believed in him who had said, "The seed of the woman will crush the head of the serpent" (Gen. 3 [15]). Then you ask, Did God introduce the law without a plan, without a definite reason, without a benefit?

The Institution of the Law

Far from it. Rather, during the time that the souls of the seed of Abraham, that is, the Jews, had been corrupted by their long stay in Egypt, to the extent that they were not only ignorant of the ancestral religion and of the covenant itself but were also going over daily more and more to Egyptian idolatry and to the entire way of worship of the Gentiles, at that time it pleased the wise and merciful Lord to come to the aid of the collapsing covenant with certain supports.

First, therefore, he (30a) restored the main points of the ancient covenant, but unfolded it more fully, and inscribed it on tablets of stone with his own finger. There is no mention, however, of ceremonies in these events up to this point. For enough had already been prescribed for the faithful. But when they continued to be unfaithful and wicked, the burden of worthless ceremonies was thrown on their shoulders, ceremonies that the patriarchs did not have. Nevertheless, it is evident that the burden was imposed for an urgent reason, for this aim and with this plan, so that they would not introduce the worship of strange gods. Therefore, God instituted his own worship, and he declared that it was pleasing to him (Psalm 50), which he actually despised, so that, with this plan, he confirmed the covenant, and in addition to that he enveloped the mystery of Christ in these ceremonies as types. Nor has this concept been created recently in our own land; rather, it has been brought to light from prophesies and gleaned from the faith of the church fathers. (30b) For Tertullian, in his *Against Marcion*, book 2,[17] says, "No one should blame God for the burden of the sacrifices, or the troublesome scrupulosities of the ceremonies, and oblations, as if he had desired such things for himself who clearly exclaimed, 'What are the multitude of your sacrifices to me and who requires them from your hands?' (Isa. 1 [11–12]). But one perceives God's diligence, by which he wished to bind together in his own religion the people, who were otherwise inclined toward idolatry and transgression, with obligations of this sort, ceremonies by which the superstition of the time was carried out, that he might call them away from these things, ordering them to be performed toward him as if he desired them, lest the people lapse into making images. But in the very ordinary transactions of life and of human relationships at home and in public, even to the care of (31a) small vessels, he marked out every detail so that, when encountering these legal disciplines everywhere, they might not at any moment be apart from the care of God." So writes Tertullian.

Now, therefore, in respect to the Decalogue and civil laws, no difference at all has arisen regarding the covenant and the people of God. For everywhere the love of God and the neighbor, faith, and love maintain the mastery. The diversity has arisen from the minds of men and from the additions foreign to the covenant, so that the covenant, which is one among all faithful people, began to be called "old" and "new," "carnal" and "spiritual," on account of certain alien elements and rather superstitious people. Indeed, it is called the "old" because the "new" follows it (as the rule of relations demands); it even promises the remission of sins, which it offers through Christ; and it also teaches faith and love. But it cannot be called "new" entirely on account of these facts, since it teaches nothing new. For it receives from the old tradition those things which we already have received (1 John 2 [7]); consequently it is called

---

17. *Adversus Marcionem* 1.18–19 in *Corpus scriptorum ecclesiasticorum latinorum* (Vindobonae, 1866–), 62:359–362 (hereafter cited as *CSEL*). Alexander Roberts and James Donaldson, eds., *The Ante-Nicene Fathers. Translations of the Writings of the Fathers Down to* A.D. *325* (Buffalo, 1885–1926), 3:311–312 (hereafter cited as *ANF*).

Tertullian (d. ca. 225) was the first great church father who wrote in Latin. In earlier writings, Bullinger depended heavily on Tertullian for patristic support on the covenant. In *The Covenant*, Bullinger quoted him here and then mentioned him later in the treatise.

Marcion, a gnostic Christian, lived in the middle of the second century. He made an absolute distinction between Judaism and Christianity. He taught that the God of the Jews and of the Old Testament was the Demiurge, who was opposed by the all-powerful, good God of the new covenant, who appeared in the person of Christ.

"new" from the fact that all the ceremonies were fulfilled by Christ, whom alone it proclaims. Since they were types and shadows of eternal things, they became obsolete. So, that ancient religion, which was thriving in that golden age of the patriarchs before the law was brought forth, now flourishes throughout the entire world, renewed and restored more fully and more clearly by Christ and made perfect with a new people, namely, the Gentiles, as though a new light had been introduced into the world. For thus also Paul (32a) speaks concerning this matter both when he addresses the Hebrews (ch. 8) and the Ephesians (ch. 2). With a similar method and plan the Scripture called carnal not those people who persevered through true faith in the covenant of God but those who depended more on carnal things than on the enduring, spiritual terms of the covenant or the promise of God. I summon Paul as a witness here, who said long ago, "For these are two covenants" (Gal. 4 [24]); he said just before that, "Tell me, you who wish to be under the law, have you listened to the law itself? For it is written that Abraham had two sons, one from a slave girl, the other from a free woman" (Gal. 4 [21]). From this we conclude that the carnal person is one who wishes to be under the law. Furthermore, not all the seed of Abraham is under the law or carnal. For he is called carnal who depends on legalities without knowledge and without the spirit and who believes firmly that he can be saved through these legalities. (32b) For ceremonies also have their own spirit, which Paul explained in detail in many passages in his letter to the Hebrews. But when they despised and did not understand the spirit and purpose of the ceremonies, they abused the law. Furthermore, the true sons of Abraham are free and they put their trust in the promises of God. Accordingly, antiquity also had the spiritual Israel. For they judge falsely who judge the whole from the part, as those who stigmatize—not without insult to the saints of God—all the fathers preceding the coming of the Lord by the name of the carnal Israel. They do not consider that this knot to be untied is a synecdoche, a common trope in Scripture. But, lest some declare that they laugh at tropes, even though we have already sufficiently established our case, I will (33a) nevertheless provide for their sake three testimonies of the greatest men in religion. Each of these men claim that Israel was a spiritual people and, what is more, that the prophets had taught the same things concerning legal matters that the apostles taught. Jeremiah, first of all, in his seventh chapter [vs. 21–23] wrote these words: "Thus says the Lord of hosts, the God of Israel: Join your burnt offerings to the sacrifices, your holocausts to the victims, and eat the meat. For I did not speak with your fathers and I did not instruct them about burnt offerings and sacrifices on the day when I led them out of Egypt; but rather I gave them this command, saying, 'Hear my voice and I will be your God and you will be my people; walk in every path I have commanded you so that it might be well with you.' " And with these words he clarifies what had (33b) been the doctrine of the prophets concerning legal matters, namely, what is the highest of all the commandments of God, the highest commandment of the covenant—obedience or faith itself. It is evident that the saints were tested by this commandment, and not by laws. Truly the Lord ordered those legal things, but with another intention by far, namely, that he might come to the aid of the collapsing covenant and that he might divert all of his own from idolatry, weld them together in faith, not that he might justify worshipers by those means but that he might foreshadow the righteousness to come, Christ. But because they were unwilling to understand, they were accused most severely by the prophet in this passage. The Lord therefore approved of the spirit and not the flesh among the Israelites. For that reason he had formed a spiritual people from the Israelites before Christ was born, because he disapproved of the carnal people so much. (34a) The most holy martyr of Christ, Stephen, in the seventh chapter of Luke's Acts of the Apostles, also proved with almost countless examples from the ancients that faith in God before the law, under the law, and after the law was pleasing to God, not ceremonies; and he established that the saints, that is, all the patriarchs and the prophets, and the righteous before the birth of Christ, worshiped God in faith and with purity of life, not with external things. Behold you have an entirely spiritual and voluntary people. Why does the apostle Paul also declare this in almost the same way in his eleventh chapter to the Hebrews with examples drawn from the patriarchs from the beginning of the world almost up to the very time of Christ? Since these men held to these things in this manner, who is there who does not see that the names "old" and "new," both of the people and of the Covenant, (34b) cannot tear asunder the very covenant and the very church of the ancient people and of our people? Even the Spirit is the same in both Testaments. But with regard to the carnal things and the transgressions of those whose sins brought them to naught in Babylon, God said that he would give a new spirit by which he meant the abundance and riches, the gift to be imparted to the faithful by Christ. We have argued the truth of this matter in our commentaries on the epistles of Peter. Up to this point I have wished to assert the unity of the covenant and to point out the reasons why it began to be called "new" and "old."

The Ways We Surpass the Ancients

Now in order that I might conceal nothing in this matter, I will briefly mention how the church of Christians, which was established after the birth of Christ, excels. (35a) First, we are indeed better off than those who lived under the law with this name because, having been freed from the entire burden of ceremonies, we have a close connection with the ancient and distinguished religion, namely, that of the patriarchs, which rested upon faith and innocence without ceremonies, that is, on the basic terms of the covenant. Second, we rejoice then in the evident truth that the shadows have been dispersed by the bright light of the gospel and that the typological foreshadowings have been fulfilled. Third then, God has made our church superior to the church of our dead fathers before the coming of Christ because we believe that the Christ has come to us, who they believed would come and whom they awaited with the greatest desire. He has given his Spirit most abundantly; he has now spread his glory throughout the whole world; and he has perfectly completed all things. (35b) For this reason, that very elderly man, Simeon, counting himself very fortunate, cries out, "Now, Lord, dismiss your servant in peace according to your word, for my eyes have seen your salvation, which you have prepared before the face of all peoples, a light for the enlightenment of the Gentiles, and the glory of your people Israel" (Luke 2 [29–32]).

Matthew, Chapter 5

Some people use Matthew 5 to object to this viewpoint. But they do not see that the Lord Jesus in that elegant and divine sermon of his did not attack either Moses or the prophets, as if they either felt or taught anything different from Christian doctrine, but he wished to correct the error of the people and to teach the true nature of the law. For the wickedness of the time and the ignorance and avarice of the Pharisees had corrupted everything. Wherefore, witnessing with eloquent words, (36a) just before he began the exposition of the law, he said, "Unless your righteousness is more abundant than that of the scribes and Pharisees, you will not be able to enter the kingdom of heaven." Therefore, Christ attacked the Pharisees, not the spirit of the law itself or of the prophets. Just a little before that he had said, "I have not come to dissolve the law but to fulfill it." Moreover, in this sermon he taught that the law was the will of God, which is entirely holy, pure, and of a most refined spirit. The law also demands the mind and the soul of humans, to the extent that it forbids covetousness. It cannot be fulfilled by humans of corrupt flesh, who do not see the plan of the whole sermon, which is to lead us to a knowledge of ourselves and to bring us (36b) to an utter denial of ourselves so that we might throw ourselves totally on the mercy of God. In the meantime, we should conform all our plans and deeds to the eternal and most pure will, that is, the law of God, not in the usual way but with the highest and most exact devotion. This and this alone is to walk carefully with the pure God (Micah 6 [8]), who is holy and wishes us also to be holy (Lev. 19 [2]).

Paul in 2 Corinthians 3

Those wandering in the same errors do not see that Paul in 2 Corinthians 3 argues against false apostles forcing legalities on the church of Christ (as he makes evident in his other epistles). For against their superstitions, nay, even their impiety, he asserts the glory of the gospel which is more illustrious than legalities. Indeed, in that passage he does not speak of the entire law (37a) but only of that part of law which is abolished. At the same time, he does not command that everything in the law and the prophets should be taken literally; but on the other hand he understands spirit not in any way you please, as is their custom, but rather as the Lord Jesus himself, who is the fulfillment of the law for the justification for all who believe (Rom. 10 [4]).

The Ebionite Mixture of Law and Gospel

Furthermore, they falsely accuse us of the Ebionite heresy.[18] Eusebius writes in this way about the Ebionites in his *Church History*, book 3, chapter 27[19]: "They feel that the law must be

---

18. The Ebionites were Jewish Christians in the early church. The Ebionites rejected Paul as an apostate; they used only the Gospel of Matthew; they saw Jesus as a man only; and they kept the Jewish Sabbath in addition to the Christian Lord's Day. Many of their teachings can be found in the writings of the earlier Qumran sect of the Dead Sea Scrolls.

19. *Historia ecclesiastica* 1.27, in J. P. Migne, ed., *Patrologiae cursus completus, Series Graeca* (Paris, 1857–1887), 20:274–275. (hereafter cited as *PG*). Philip Schaff and Henry Wace, eds., *A Select Library of Nicene and Post-Nicene Fathers of the Christian Church, Second Series* (New York, 1890–1900), 1:159 (hereafter cited as *PNF2*).

kept, and they do not think that faith alone in Christ is sufficient for salvation (as I have said, they mix together legal things with gospel). Therefore they keep the fleshly observance of the law. Moreover, at the same time they reject all the epistles of the apostle, and they call him an apostle of the law." (37b) Nor did Irenaeus,[20] Tertullian, or Augustine[21] report anything different. Wherefore our doctrine of the single and eternal covenant of God, and of the abrogation of legalities, is far different from their blasphemy. There is no one who does not already know this.

Deuteronomy, Chapter 5

But what will we say to the words of the Lord in this passage of Moses in Deuteronomy, chapter 5 [2–3]? "The Lord our God made a covenant with us on Horeb; not with our fathers did the Lord enter into this covenant but with us who exist and live at the present time." Augustine in his commentary on Deuteronomy, chapter 5, question 9,[22] explains this text as a synecdoche. He understands these fathers to be those whom God struck down in the desert. (38a) "They," he says, "who did not enter into the land of the promise do not belong to this covenant, but their sons did belong, I say, if they who were not over twenty years old when God had spoken on the mountain, so that at that time they could not be counted in a census. Nevertheless they could have been nineteen years of age or less all the way to boyhood, in which case they could have seen and heard and retained in memory all those things which were said and done." Moreover, Johannes Oecolampadius, in his published commentary on Jeremiah, explains it almost in the same way: "Before God, that eternal covenant which is arranged differently according to the diversity of the times is one. And also in relation

---

20. Irenaeus (d. ca. 200) was bishop of Lyons. He seems to have had some real influence on the development of Bullinger's covenant theology. But Bullinger mentioned Irenaeus only twice in connection with the covenant in his early writings. This is the second reference. The first is in *De origine erroris, in divorum ac simulachrorum cultu* (Basel, 1529), sig. Bii(v), where he also referred to Tertullian, Lactantius, Eusebius, and Augustine as fathers who taught the covenant. For Bullinger's use of the fathers and their influence on the development of his covenant thought, see Baker, *Bullinger and the Covenant*, pp. 19–23.

21. Aurelius Augustine (354–430), bishop of Hippo, had the greatest influence of any church father on Bullinger. Augustine was involved in several doctrinal controversies. His writings against the Donatists and the Pelagians had a particularly important impact upon the theology of the Protestant Reformers.

22. *Quaestionum in Heptateuchum libri VII* 5.9 (*CSEL* 28, 2:374–375).

to the inner human realities, it always has been one and will remain one, not only as it is in eternal predestination. . . . (38b) Notice, however, the great diversity of the covenants. The Lord made a pact with Abraham with words and demanded nothing except obedience from him. But under Moses many strange and dreadful things were added, things known not only to the one leader but things evident to all the people. Then it was fortified with so many circumstantial legalities, all of which return to those ten words of the tablet of the covenant."[23]

The Promise of the Land of Canaan

Now the objection is easily disposed of that the land of Canaan, wars and victories, Judaic glory and happiness, are things least suited to the ways of Christians, for whom nothing awaits except the cross and exile, in as much as the Scripture says about them, "All who wish to live piously in Christ will endure persecution" (2 Tim. 3 [12]).

For no one denies that the promise of the land (39a) of Canaan was bound to a specific place; but neither can anyone deny that the same promise or rather a similar promise of earthly things was made equally to all the Gentiles. In fact, Abraham himself, to whom the promise of the land of Canaan was made, did not (as Stephen said in Acts 7 [5]) even put the mark of his foot on the land; but in the meantime, he acquired great wealth, just as his posterity, Isaac, Jacob, and Joseph, did. For even though they did not take possession of the promised land, they were nevertheless very famous because of their riches. Now I believe that this was done by the Lord as an example for all the Gentiles, from which they might learn that they also would lack nothing if they feared the Lord after the manner of the patriarchs. And you will find many more promises of this type throughout both Testaments (Psalm 37; Matt. 6 [25–34]; Acts 14 [17]; and 17 [26–28]; Heb. 13 [5–6]). (39b) In respect to the happiness of the fathers, however, it is certain that they hardly enjoyed a perfectly good fortune in these

---

23. Johannes Oecolampadius, *In Hieremiam prophetam commentariorem libri tres* (Argentinae, 1533), sigs. Rii–Rii(v). As indicated in the text, Bullinger deleted several lines from Oecolampadius. Oecolampadius was not as supportive as Bullinger would have the reader believe. Although the passage quoted by Bullinger seems to support his view of only one covenant, the material preceding and following, as well as the portion deleted, supports a two covenant scheme, old and new, carnal and spiritual, corresponding with law and gospel (Oecolampadius, *In Hieremiam*, sigs. Ri–Riii(v)).

lands. In fact, they entered the kingdom of God by means of the cross and many tribulations.

The Cross, Peace and Victory of the Saints

Everyone knows how many trials Abraham endured in the course of that journey, so I need not call to mind the rest of the details. The patriarch Jacob never enjoyed any good fortune that was not soured by various severe hardships. There is no reason for me to relate any details about Moses, Joshua, Samuel, David, and all the other distinguished figures. No single one of them would suffice as an example in enumerating their many hardships, calamities, and labors undertaken for the sake of the Lord. Even the sacred writers themselves have scarcely been able to relate everything in their many books. What about the fact that (40a) the faithful people of Judah endured no less persecutions on account of their piety and faith, sometimes from their own wicked kings, sometimes from foreign tyrants, than the church of Christ itself suffered from the impious and blasphemous Caesars? For as this church has Nero, Domitian, Maxentius, Julian, Decian, Severus, Valerian, and Diocletian, so the ancient church had Pharaoh, Ahab, Joash, Manasseh, Jehoiachim, Zedekiah, Nebuchadnezzar, and Antiochus. Truly the priests and prophets of the ancient church deserved to be made examples for Christian martyrs. For the Lord even said so in the Gospel of Matthew: "Blessed are they who suffer persecution for the sake of righteousness, for theirs is the kingdom (40b) of heaven. Blessed are you when men shall attack you on account of me. Rejoice and exult, because your reward in heaven is great. For in this way did they persecute the prophets before you" (Matt. 5 [10–12]). On the other hand, there is no doubt that there have always been myriads of saints who have lived piously in Christ, who were never sent into exile or killed for the sake of the faith. Therefore Paul's statement, "All who wish to live piously in Christ will suffer persecution" (2 Tim. 3 [12]), does not refer to a common occurrence, but is a consolation for the afflicted. There are also different kinds of persecution.[24] Not only does he who is thrown into prison or hung from a tree endure persecution but also he who (41a) is tested by different adversities and temptations. The latter customarily happens to pious people otherwise

---

24. Here Bullinger made a marginal reference to Augustine's *Contra Gaudentius Donistarum Episcopum* 2.13 (*CSEL* 53:272–274). Gaudentius (d. A.D. 410) was the Donatist Bishop of Brescia. Augustine wrote this work about A.D. 420.

enjoying peace and security of mind. For even the apostle Paul, most often safe from the snares and furies of persecutors and, what is more, revived by the ministrations of the brethren, experienced severe anxieties of the soul. For the soul of a Christian is also affected by another person's distress. Wherefore the apostle said, "Who is weakened and I am not weakened? Who is offended and I am not distressed?" (2 Cor. 11 [29]; see also Rom. 12 [15] and Heb. 13 [3]). Moreover, the most holy prophet Isaiah in those chapters in which he describes the church being gathered together from the whole world, into which church he said that kings also would come, did not teach that the church should in every way and always be exposed to slaughters, so that on this earth it would be without any kind of peace, happiness, and victory (Isa. 49 [1–7]). And Doctor Aurelius (41b) Augustine in his work *The City of God*, book 5, in the final chapters,[25] offered pleasant and useful accounts for the reader about the victories and wonderful happiness of certain Christian kings. Likewise in *Against the Manichean Faustus*, book 22, from chapters 74 to 80,[26] he discusses war and the right of war in many passages, but we do not intend to consider this matter further. Up to this point, we have wished to explain what the conditions of the covenant are, that this covenant is one and eternal, and for what reasons the nomenclature "old" and "new" was adopted. Now we will include a few remarks about the ceremony and the sacrament of the covenant.

The Sacrament of the Covenant

Circumcision

Those who entered into covenants took either a ram, a heifer, or a she-goat, cut it into two parts, then passed through between the parts, (42a) testifying that if they did not stand firm by the pacts, God then should in the same manner split them in two and do away with them entirely. Indications of this rite are seen in Genesis 15 [10] and Jeremiah 34 [15]. Alluding to this human custom, therefore, God consecrates the covenant with blood and adds an explanation in plain words, saying, "And the uncircumcised male, the foreskin of whose flesh shall

---

25. *De civitate Dei* 5.24–26 (*CSEL* 40, 1:260–266; *PNF* 2:104–107).

26. *Contra Faustum* 22.74–80 (*CSEL* 25:671–683; *PNF* 4:300–305). Faustus of Mileve was a Manichaean leader in Carthage. Augustine's treatise against him was an answer to a polemic that Faustus had written against Christianity about A.D. 400.

not have been circumcised, his soul shall be blotted out from his people" (Gen. 17 [14a]). That which must be understood not only concerning the cut-off foreskin, but more so of the entire covenant, is that he who shall have neglected this covenant must be destroyed by an eternal curse. The reason for this follows: "Because he has made my covenant void and broken it" (Gen. 17 [14b]). Moreover, he who has broken it, through contempt of God's covenant and institution, despises the sacrament of God as useless; or, even if he does not (42b) despise the sign of the covenant which he has received, he nevertheless forsakes the covenant itself by faithlessness and moral impurity.

Infants Dying Without the Sign of the Covenant

Wherefore we conclude that infants who are born of faithful parents and who die either before they have begun to live or before they could be inscribed among the people of God with the sacred sign of the covenant cannot be damned with the support of this text. For God is speaking of despisers of the covenant who are adults. Which fact the words themselves demonstrate sufficiently, stating the matter in this way: "And the uncircumcised male on whose flesh the foreskin shall not have been circumcised, his soul shall be banished from his people," etc. We believe, moreover, such infants to be saved by the grace and mercy of God, by whom they are not prejudged as by those who judge them only according to the rites of the church. (43a)

Circumcision also had another mystery. For Paul says, "A testament takes effect only in death; it is not yet valid while the testator is living" (Heb. 9 [17]). God, however, is the testator; therefore it behooved God to die. And since he is immutable and immortal, he assumed the seed of Abraham and, in the assumed flesh, he suffered, shed his blood, and in that way, as I would express it, ratified the testament. Moreover, in order that he might hand down this mystery to the fathers in a figure, he willed that the seed of Abraham itself be circumcised, signifying that the true seed of Abraham, Christ the Lord, would confirm that covenant by his death and blood.

The New Sacraments

For this reason, the Lord Jesus himself, speaking in Matthew's Gospel about the sacrament of the new covenant, said, "This is my blood (43b) which is of the new covenant, which is shed for many for the remission of sins" (Matt. 26 [28]). Hence-

forth, it was also necessary for the old sacrament to be changed
and the new to be instituted. For after everything was fulfilled
by the death of Christ and the covenant itself had been confirmed, certainly those signs which prefigured the future death
of Christ had to be changed and, in their place, signs substituted that, with their meaning, signify the completion of the most
perfect justification. That is what we attribute to the mystery of
Baptism and the Eucharist. For these sacraments, instituted by
God, became for the people of the new testament symbols of
the covenant and of divine grace already confirmed through
Christ. Thereafter, circumcision meant that one must cut off
the foreskin of the heart and serve God (44a) in the obedience
of faith (Deut. 10 [16]; Jer. 4 [4]). Therefore circumcision was
given to those to whom the grace and the covenant of God was
first offered, through the assistance and the institution of God
who did not scorn being the God of little children and who also
first offered himself to us out of sheer grace and said, "I will be
your God." Then by that same circumcision God bound the
faithful to himself, commanding that they adhere to him in
faith and innocence. From all of this it is also evident that the
entire covenant was contained in the sacrament of the covenant; in the same manner, the entire essence of the renewed
covenant is contained in our sacraments, Baptism and the
Eucharist. Truly to examine these things fully at the present
time would pull us farther away from our purpose. For it
already shall have been enough that God indicated in instituting the sacrament of the covenant that he wished to consider
(44b) the customs of mortals who, since they exist not only in
soul but also in body, are often led by means of visible things
and signs into the contemplation of invisible things. Therefore
God gave the sacraments, which the ancients called the visible
signs of invisible grace. Further, he gave circumcision and the
Passover to the ancients, but to us who are his people after
Christ suffered, he gave Baptism and the Eucharist. And for
the rest, what is visible and invisible in these sacraments and
what is their power and efficacy, it has been dealt with elsewhere. Now we shall speak about the records.

The Documents of the Covenant

The final step in making testaments or covenants is the
composition of documents, or, if you prefer, records, compre-
hending and transmitting to posterity the entire essence and
testimony of the matter transacted.

But these records (45a) were also chosen as the names of the covenant or testament. For we refer to the written records of the covenant or testament as the covenant or the testament itself, when in truth they are not the covenant or the testament but only the exposition of the conditions and the testimony of the entire transaction. The Lord did not bother to have any records written for the ancient patriarchs, for they bore the covenant in their hearts, inscribed by the finger of God. But to their posterity God gave what they longed for—the entire true religion received from their fathers, almost as from hand to hand, carved on stone tablets by Moses, which he called the records of the covenant and the testament, undoubtedly with that plan and for that reason which we have already explained. Later, lest anyone might find (45b) anything lacking, he imposed on Moses himself, then on the prophets, and eventually on the apostles of the Lord, the duty to write fitting and complete books about this matter. From the very contents of these books, they have deserved the title "Old" and "New" Testament among all peoples in every age. Undoubtedly this is true also because they explain abundantly how that covenant entered into with Abraham was to be kept by the ancient people and how that covenant led them to life under the hope of the Christ to come through various means, types, and ways in religion. Truly these books teach how the covenant was renewed and consecrated in a new way by Christ, how all the types were fulfilled through him, and how a new people, namely, the multitude of the Gentiles, was called into the unity of faith, (46a) and established in the true religion, and led into eternal life through Christ. These are books of such truth and righteousness that all learned and holy men of all ages have believed that eternal life and the faith of the worshipers of the true God could be firmly established on their teachings. For Isaiah cries out, "If they shall say to you, 'Consult the sorcerers, the diviners, the soothsayers, those who do incantations,' should not every people consult its gods about the living as well as the dead? Hasten even more, therefore, to the law and to the testimony" (Isa. 8 [19–20]). Then Christ the Lord says, "They have Moses and the prophets, let them listen to them; and if they do not listen to them, neither will they believe if someone rose from the dead" (Luke 16 [29, 31]).

Later on, if any dispute arises among the heirs about an inheritance, they immediately consult the records (46b) for themselves and thus they place their confidence in these witnesses, in order that they might do everything according to the rule of the records. In the same way, if any strife arises in the matter of religion about the true or false worship of God, let us consult the records of the covenant, the books of each Testament. Let us believe them, let us establish everything according to these books. For the two greatest lights of our religion, David in Psalm 19 and Paul in 2 Timothy 3, testify abundantly that all piety and righteousness have been perfectly embraced in these books.

Epilogue

The Antiquity of the Christian Religion

Such are the thoughts, most splendid readers, that I wanted to share with you concerning the one and eternal testament or covenant of God. Truly, those things which belong to this covenant—its conditions, the place and purpose of its sacrament, and what is commanded by its records—have been put together by me by virtue of grace from the Lord. (47a) I have done so partly in order that I might serve the brothers who so often earnestly request such an exposition from us and partly for those whose great depravity requires it. Then too, I have done so partly in order that I might indicate in passing the clarity, simplicity, and antiquity of the Scripture and of our religion, which today is ill-spoken of by many people, as if it were heretical. Indeed, the oldest religion of the Gentiles is idolatry, or the worship of images. It is, in fact, older than great men of fame may otherwise compute. For there are those who in the times of Jupiter, or a little before, believed that the temples were established for the worship of new gods. But the opinion of Herodotus[27] in his second book of histories and of Strabo[28] in the seventeenth book of his Geography appear to be more probable. These men (47b) asserted that the Egyptians were the first worshipers and the creators of the gods, from whom the rest of the nations accepted idolatry. But to those who diligently compute dates, it is clear that Jupiter is younger than Moses by several centuries. But Moses testified not only that the Jewish people, steeped in idolatry in Egypt according to the example of the Egyptians, set up an image to the god Apis in the desert but also that the zeal for idolatry flourished in the times of the patriarchs. Now the Jewish religion, which I understand to be defined in time by circumcision and laws, is also ancient, seeing that it began partly in the time of Abraham

---

27. Herodotus, *Histories* 2.37–76, in *Herodotus*, with an English translation by S. D. Godley, 4 vols., Loeb Classical Library (Cambridge, Mass., 1981), 1:319–363.

28. Strabo, *Geography* 17.1–2, in *The Geography of Strabo*, with an English translation by Horace Leonard Jones, 8 vols., Loeb Classical Library (London, 1932), 8:2–153.

and partly in the time of Moses. But the Christian religion is older by far than such things. For Abraham is declared justified in the sacred Scripture before he was circumcised. (48a) There are also those prior to Abraham—Noah, Enoch, Seth, Abel, Adam—who pleased God through faith without circumcision. It is annoying that in the present day the Turkish and papal religions are counted as examples of ancient religions. But it was not many centuries ago, about the year A.D. 630, that the former issued from its most corrupt and impious founder, Mohammed,[29] who blasphemed the truth. And the papal religion, scarcely any older than Islam, obscured the precepts of Christ, the prophetic tradition, and the apostolic simplicity, purity, and truth. While I say nothing here about that faith which, comprised in twelve articles, they confess by mouth together with us, I do speak about the papal dogmas and religious customs which they trust as most certain, ancient, and infallible. (48b) Some examples are masses, images, monasticism, and many other things that were unknown in the primitive holy church of God. For Albert the Great,[30] the chief of the scholastic theologians, referred to Gregory,[31] the first Roman pontiff of that name, who lived around A.D. 600, as the originator of the mass. This same Gregory declared in a certain letter to Bishop Serenus of Marseilles[32] (I use Gregory's own words) that antiquity permitted stories to be painted in the venerable churches of the saints for the instruction of ignorant people. I do not know how he understood antiquity, but I do know this, that the famous Lactantius Firmianus,[33] a contemporary of Constantine the Great,[34] said in eloquent words, "There is no

---

29. Mohammed (A.D. 570–632) was the founder of Mohammedanism, or Islam, and the author of the sacred writings of Islam, the Koran.

30. Albert the Great (1193–1280) was the founder of the high scholastic theology of the middle and late thirteenth century. It was Albert, along with his student Thomas Aquinas, who substituted Aristotelian logic and metaphysics for the Platonic and Neoplatonic ideas that had flourished for so long in the Middle Ages.

31. Gregory I, pope from 590 to 604, was probably not the originator of the Gregorian Chant, and he certainly did not create the mass.

32. Serenus, bishop of Marseilles from about 595 to 600, is known only by letters from Gregory I. After Serenus had broken the images in the churches of Marseilles, Gregory wrote to him that the paintings and images in the churches were there to instruct the illiterate. While commending his opposition to idolatry, Gregory deplored his violence. Serenus ignored the pope's admonitions and received a severe rebuke.

33. Lucius Caecilius Firmianus Lactantius lived in the late third and early fourth centuries. He was the teacher of Crispus, the son of Constantine.

34. Constantine the Great, emperor from 306 to 337, was the first Christian emperor. He was converted to Christianity in 312 and issued the Edict of Milan, an edict of toleration for Christians, in 313.

doubt that there is no religion at all (49a) wherever there are images." This is close to the opinion of the Holy Bishop Epiphanius of Salamina[35] in Cyprus, on the basis of whose view expositor Dr. Jerome[36] declared publicly that human images were placed in the church of Christ against the authority of Scripture and against our religion. And Dr. Jerome, according to the authors Eutropius[37] and Prosper of Aquitaine,[38] died in the year A.D. 422. How then could Gregory use "antiquity" in defense of painting in the sanctuaries? Even if he could have brought forth the strongest support for such "antiquity," nevertheless the prophet of the Lord, speaking with irony about images, says, "Should they not teach you?" (Hab. 2 [19]) In fact, Gregory himself assailed the worship of images in that very same letter of his. (49b) Nevertheless, the popes have not only allowed such worship but (49b) have even ordered it. And Benedict,[39] abbot of Cassino, whom all monks call "Father," flourished only a little before the time of Gregory, perhaps sixty years if the supposition of Bede[40] about the calculation of the times is correct. For Jerome remembered that Paul and Anthony[41] did nothing to defend pontifical monasticism. Now really, if you compare these times with ancient times, you will find that the papal religion is an utterly new thing and in no way ought it to be compared to earlier antiquity. But even though such people prefer this religion above all others, and many things are invented about its antiquity and certitude, we

_____

35. Epiphanius (ca. 320–404) was elected bishop of Constantia, the ancient Salamis, in Cyprus in 367. He was a severe critic of Origen, whose interest in ancient Greek philosophy he saw as the source of many errors.

36. Jerome (d. ca. 420) was one of the greatest of the church fathers and a prolific author. His writings include biblical commentaries, histories, dogmatic and polemical works, and letters. His most lasting work, *The Vulgate,* was his Latin translation of the Bible, which became scripture for the entire West for over a thousand years.

37. It is not possible to identify this Eutropius. He cannot be Eutropius the Roman historian who was undoubtedly dead before 422.

38. Prosper of Aquitaine (d. after 455) was a champion of Augustine's theology, especially his doctrine of predestination, against the nascent semi-Pelagianism in the area of Marseilles.

39. Benedict of Nursia (fl. 530s and 540s) was the founder of the monastery of Cassino, perhaps in 529, and was also the founder of the Benedictine Order.

40. The Venerable Bede (ca. 672–735) was the first great English scholar. He wrote *The Ecclesiastical History of the English People,* among other historical works.

41. Bullinger's reference here is to Jerome's *"Vita pauli,"* a biography of his friend Paul of Thebes, whom he considered the first hermit. Jerome wrote the *Vita,* probably in the late 370s, as a celebration of Paul's one hundredth birthday. The other reference is to Anthony, born in Egypt about 250, who is featured in the *"Vita pauli"* as a younger man whom Paul met in the desert. Anthony is usually considered the first Christian hermit and the founder of monasticism. For the *Vita pauli,* see *PL* 23:17–28.

glory far more justly in the antiquity of our faith, inasmuch as it is older than the religions of both the Gentiles and the Jews. It has endured from the beginning of the world to (50a) this very day, about 6,733 years. From the birth of Christ up to the present day, 1,534 years are computed, and from the beginning of the world to the birth of our Lord, 5,199 years.[42] We have proven that the faith of Abraham, Adam, and Christ was the same. But also Eusebius in the first book of his *Church History*, chapter 1,[43] asserts the same thing that we do. It will not be annoying to include his words, although we cannot include all of them. The passage is rather long, but for many reasons it deserves to be read diligently.

The Christian or Evangelical Faith, the Oldest of All

Eusebius says, "All those who are written down in the order of generation from Abraham all the way back to the first man were truly Christian in deeds and in religion, if not in name. The name 'Christian' indicates the fact that the one who believes in Christ holds to his (50b) teaching, faith, piety, and justice; devotedly adheres to divine wisdom; and pursues everything that leads to virtue. If these things are indicated by the meaning of the name 'Christian,' and designate this person as a follower of the true religion, then those holy men, of whom we have spoken above, are also acknowledged to have been Christians. Corporal circumcision did not exist with them, nor did the observance of the Sabbath (just as we do not observe it). Neither did they have any scruples about regulations regarding food, or the rest of the practices handed down to their posterity by Moses to be observed typologically and spiritually. Therefore, since there were those men who were religious without all of these observances, of whom we made mention above, who followed the faith of him whom we (51a) now follow, the faith of Christ, who frequently appeared to them and taught them those things which pertain to faith and piety, which we have established earlier, how can anyone doubt that the origin of this people commenced with those men and has been traced downward in time from them? They followed the same God, the author and guide of life, and they persisted in similar religious

---

42. Bullinger corrected this date in another, somewhat later, publication, where he gave the date of creation as 3969 B.C. (*Epitome temporum et rerum ab orbe condito, ad primum usque annum Iothan regis Iudae* [Zurich, 1565], fol. 97b).
43. It was chapter 4 of book 1, rather than chapter 1, *Historia ecclesiastica* 1.4 (*PG* 20, cols. 74–79; *PNF2* 1:87–88).

observances. And finally, this religion was so far pre-sent and pre-formed in them that they were not even considered strangers to the name itself (which certainly seems to make the only distinction); indeed, not only are they already at that time declared to be 'Christians' but also, with divine eloquence, they are called 'Christs.' "[44] And after certain other arguments, Eusebius concludes, "The religion of Christians is neither a new nor a foreign one, (51b) nor has it arisen recently. Rather, since we are permitted freely to indicate what is the truth, it was the first religion of all, originating with the very beginning of the world, from the beginning receiving shape and form by the same Christ as God, creator, and teacher." So far have I recounted the words of Saint Eusebius.

Now I ask, therefore, who is ashamed of or regrets the most difficult labors undertaken on behalf of the covenant of God, since it is now evident that from the beginning of the world all the saints have worshiped God in this covenant and have even laid down their lives on behalf of it? Who has not been greatly fortified, even though sweating in the midst of great labors, by the fact that the eternal God has bound himself to us by an eternal oath and has most faithfully kept that eternal covenant with all (52a) his saints from the beginning? For often the saints have been thrown into dangers, often religion itself has been threatened with destruction, and more often it seemed to be defeated and buried, and even God was quite frequently thought to have deserted his own people. But rising up at the right moment, God has always protected the true religion, having defeated and crushed the impious ones. This same God is immutable and eternal. This same God, therefore, even today will not fail those of his own who are bound to him in the eternal covenant, no matter how the world might be seized with madness. To him be the glory!

Psalm 25:10
All the paths of the Lord are grace and faith to those who keep his testament and his covenant!

1534

---

44. This is a reference to 1 Chron. 16:22 and Ps. 55:15.

Notes

Introduction

1. Ketcham, "James Madison and the Nature of Man," pp. 62–76.
2. Torrance, "Strengths and Weaknesses of the Westminster Theology," p. 48.

Chapter 1: Heinrich Bullinger and the Origins of the Federal Tradition

1. Friedrich, *Trends of Federalism*, p. 6.
2. For example, see Jürgen Moltmann and Elisabeth Moltmann-Wendel, *Humanity in God* (New York: Friendship Press, 1983).
3. Friedrich, *Trends of Federalism*, p. 7.
4. For a more extensive discussion of ideas of these church fathers, see Baker, *Bullinger and the Covenant*, pp. 19–23.
5. Oberman, "The Shape of Late Medieval Thought," p. 15. On the nominalist *pactum*, see also Oberman's *Harvest of Medieval Theology* and "Wir sind pettler," pp. 232–252.
6. Heinrich Bullinger, *Anklag und ernstliches ermanen Gottes Allmaechtigen/zuo eyner gemeynenn Eydgnoschafft/das sy sich vonn jren Sünden zuo jmm keere* (Zurich, 1528), sig. Cii(v), Cvi.
7. For an estimate of Bullinger's influence on the Reformed tradition and a complete study of his covenantal thought, see Baker, *Bullinger and the Covenant*.
8. There is no biography of Bullinger in English. Schulthess-Rechberg, *Heinrich Bullinger der Nachfolger Zwinglis*, is the most recent biography. Fritz Blanke's 1942 study of the young Bullinger (*Der junge Bullinger 1504–1531*), which covers his life only up to his move to Zurich, is again available: Blanke and Leuschner, *Heinrich Bullinger: Vater der reformierten Kirche* (1990). Leuschner has added vignettes

)

139

about Bullinger's work in Zurich. Although Leuschner's additions do not make the book a complete biography, they supply useful information for the modern reader.

9. For a more detailed description of Bullinger's reaction to the events of the period 1531–1535, see J. Wayne Baker, "Church, State, and Dissent: The Crisis of the Swiss Reformation, 1531-1536," *Church History* 57 (1988): 135–152.

10. Ulrich Gäbler, et al., eds., *Heinrich Bullinger, Werke. 2, Abt.: Briefwechsel,* 4 vols. (Zurich, 1973–1989), 3:220; 3:239 (hereafter cited as *HBBW*).

11. Emil Arbenz and Hermann Wartmann, eds., *Vadianische Briefsammlung,* 7 vols. (St. Gallen, 1890–1913), 5:186.

12. "H. Bullinger an Heinrich Simler von dem Touff." undated (late November–early December 1525), Zurich Zentralbibliothek, MS. A82, fols. 75r–81r; "De institutione et genuino eucharistiae usu epistola," 10 December 1525, Zurich Zentralbibliothek, MS. A82, fols. 81r–89r; "Uff D. Iohansen Burckardi predigers ze Bremgartten gespraechbuechlin, antwort Heilrychen Bullinger die Geschrifft und Mess betraeffende," undated (1527–early 1528), Zurich Zentralbibliothek, MS. A82, fols. 56v–73v.

13. Bullinger to Matthias Schmid, 8 February 1526, *HBBW* 1:98–99; Bullinger to Johannes Enzlin, 27 February 1526, *HBBW* 1:110–111; Bullinger to Anna Adlischwyler (his fiancée), 24 February 1528, *HBBW* 1:153–155.

14. Heinrich Bullinger, *Von dem unverschampten fraefel ergerlichem verwyrren/ unnd unwarhafftem leeren/ der selbsgesandten Widertoeuffern* (Zurich, 1531).

15. The covenant is a prominent feature in Bullinger's commentaries; in fact, the present treatise, *The Covenant,* is appended to his commentary on the epistles of Paul and the other apostles. *In omnes apostolicas epistolas, divi videlicet Pauli XIIII., et VII. canonicas,* 2 vols. (Zurich, 1537). Bullinger highlighted the covenant in *Der alt gloub* (Zurich, 1537); *Summa Christenlicher Religion* (Zurich, 1556); *Catechesis pro adultioribus scripta, de his potissimum* (Zurich, 1559); *Isaias excellentissimus Dei propheta* (Zurich, 1567); and in many other writings.

16. Korff, *Die Anfänge,* p. 15.

17. For a fuller treatment of the development of Zwingli's covenant idea and the difference between him and Bullinger, see Baker, *Bullinger and the Covenant,* pp. 1–19.

18. See ibid., pp. 186–189, for a fuller treatment of Oecolampadius on the covenant.

19. See ibid., pp. 189–191, for a discussion of Bucer on the covenant, and for mention of Martin Cellarius and Wolfgang Capito, neither of whom can be regarded as a covenant theologian.

20. For a fuller treatment of Musculus, see ibid., pp. 200–202.

Rolston, *John Calvin Versus the Westminster Confession,* wrongly assumes that Musculus's general and special covenants were an early expression of the later distinction between the covenant of works and the covenant of grace. This development of federal theology must be attributed to Ursinus, with his covenant of nature and covenant of grace. For Musculus, the general covenant was simply God's promise never again to destroy life on earth with a flood.

21. For the most recent study, see Lillback, "The Binding of God: Calvin's Role in the Development of Covenant Theology." For other bibliography, see Baker, *Bullinger and the Covenant,* p. 259.

22. A more detailed treatment of Calvin on the covenant and the differences between Calvin and Bullinger can be found in Baker, *Bullinger and the Covenant,* pp. 193–198; for Augustine on testament and covenant, see pp. 19–20.

23. See Rolston, *John Calvin Versus the Westminster Confession.*

24. Weir, *The Origins of Federal Theology in Sixteenth-Century Reformation Thought,* pp. 99–101.

25. Heinrich Bullinger, *Der alt gloub,* sig. Avi; cf. *Sermonum Decades quinque* (Zurich, 1552), III:x, fols. 163b–164 (hereafter cited as *Decades*).

26. Bullinger, *Der alt gloub,* sigs. Avii–Aviii(v).

27. Bullinger, *Summa Christenlicher Religion,* fols. 2b, 31–31b.

28. For a detailed discussion of Bullinger's teaching on predestination, see Baker, *Bullinger and the Covenant,* pp. 27–54.

29. For discussion of Gomarus and Perkins, see ibid., pp. 205–207.

30. See McCoy, *Covenant Theology of Cocceius.*

31. See Armstrong, *Calvinism and the Amyraut Heresy.*

32. Pettit, *The Heart Prepared: Grace and Conversion in Puritan Spiritual Life.*

33. See Baker, *Bullinger and the Covenant,* passim; and idem, "In Defense of Magisterial Discipline: Bullinger's 'Tractatus de excommunicatione' of 1568," 1:141–159.

34. Laski, *A Defense of Liberty Against Tyrants;* and Franklin, *Constitutionalism and Resistance;* pp. 146–199. The standard biography of Mornay is Patry, *Philippe du Plessis-Mornay: Un huguenot homme d'état.*

35. Carney, *Politics.*

Chapter 2: The Development
of the Federal Theological Tradition

1. See Heinrich Bullinger, *Werke,* vol. 1, for a detailed listing of the various editions of his publications in different languages. See also Walter Hollweg, *Heinrich Bullingers Hausbuch: Eine Untersuchung über die Anfänge der reformierten Predigtliteratur.* The *Decades* became required reading for clergy in the province of Lincoln in 1577 and in

the province of Canterbury in 1586. See David Keep, "Bullinger's *Decades* in England" (unpublished paper, 14 August 1975).

2. The Dutch title is *Der Leken Wechwyser*.

3. See Korff, *Die Anfänge*, p. 31; Schrenk, *Gottesreich und Bund*, p. 51; and Van t'Hooft, *De theologie van Heinrich Bullinger in betrekking tot de Nederlandsche Reformatie*, pp. 130–204.

4. Quoted in Baker, *Bullinger and the Covenant*, p. 211.

5. The abbreviated Latin title is *Methodica descriptio . . . de gratuito Dei foedere* (Leiden, 1584).

6. Quoted in Korff, *Die Anfänge*, p. 41 n. 52.

7. See Baker, *Bullinger and the Covenant*, pp. 212–213.

8. L. Knappert, *Geschiedenis der Nederlandsche Hervormde Kerk gedurende de 16e en 17e Eeuw*, 2 vols. (Amsterdam, 1911), 1:125.

9. Arminius had studied in Geneva and became an eminent pastor in Amsterdam before taking on, in 1603, the additional duties of a professorship in theology at Leiden. It was in the latter position that he was subjected to the accusations of his colleague, Gomarus, and gave his name to a movement that opposed the high Calvinist views on predestination and human free will. For further information, see Bangs, *Arminius: A Study in the Dutch Reformation*.

10. *The newe Testament* (1534). "W. T. to the Reader," sigs. *.iii–*.iiii.

11. For further discussion of the possible influence from Zurich on Tyndale, see Baker, *Bullinger and the Covenant*, pp. 208–209; and Moeller, "The Beginnings of Puritan Covenant Theology," p. 54.

12. See the preface to *Biblia, the bible that is holy scrypture*. Tr. out of the Douche and Latyn (Zurich [?], 1535). For additional information on the Coverdale-Bullinger connection, see Baker, *Bullinger and the Covenant*, p. 209.

13. "Unto the Christian Reader," in *Early Writings of John Hooper, D. D. Lord Bishop of Gloucester and Worcester, Martyr, 1555*, edited by Samuel Carr (Cambridge, 1858), pp. 255–257; see also pp. 271–272, 282–283, and 415.

14. The text of the Heidelberg Catechism can be found in Schaff, *The Creeds of Christendom*, 3:307–355.

15. Zacharias Ursinus, *Opera theologica*, 1:10; quoted in Heppe, *Geschichte des Pietismus*, p. 210n.

16. Zacharias Ursinus, *Doctrinae Christianae compendium*, pp. 3, 7.

17. Ibid., pp. 225–226; quoted in Baker, *Bullinger and the Covenant*, p. 202.

18. See Heppe, *Reformed Dogmatics*, pp. 325–327.

19. Ursinus, *Opera theologica*, 1:10; quoted in David A. Weir, *Foedus Naturale: The Origins of Federal Theology in Sixteenth-Century Reformation Thought* (Ph. D. diss., Saint Andrews, 1984), p. 123.

20. See Bierma, *German Calvinism in the Confessional Age,* for more details on the life and federal thought of Olevianus.

21. Quoted in Sepp, *Het Godgeleerd Onderwijs in Nederland,* 1:19.

22. Heppe, *Geschichte des Pietismus,* p. 210.

23. Diestel, "Studien zur Föderaltheologie," p. 213.

24. Trinterud, "The Origins of Puritanism," pp. 37–57.

25. McGiffert, "From Moses to Adam," p. 136.

26. Quoted in ibid., p. 136.

27. William Perkins, *Werkes,* 3 vols. (London, 1626), 1:32.

28. Ibid., 1:70.

29. Ibid., 1:164f.

30. Ibid., 1:610f.

31. Ibid., 2:74f.

32. Robert Rollock, *Select Works,* edited by William M. Gunn, 2 vols. (Edinburgh, 1849), 1:34–38 and *passim.*

33. The title of this work is *De triplici Dei cum homines foedere theses.* For additional information on Cameron's life and thought, see Armstrong, *Calvinism and the Amyraut Heresy,* pp. 42–70.

34. See Moltmann, "Prädestination und Heilsgeschichte bei Moyse Amyraut," p. 271.

35. See Armstrong, *Calvinism and the Amyraut Heresy,* p. 266.

Chapter 3: Federal Political Philosophy: Mornay and Althusius

1. See, for example, Delbert Hillers, *The Covenant: The History of a Biblical Idea* (Baltimore: Johns Hopkins Press, 1969). The title is misleading. The book is not the history of the biblical idea of covenant. Instead, it is a careful account of the history of the idea of covenant in the Bible. If Hillers is aware of the important and influential history of this biblical idea in the centuries during which the modern Western world was taking shape, he gives no hint of it in this book.

2. Inaccurate views of the history of the perspectives underlying the political and social institutions of Western society undermine the validity of analyses of the problems of the contemporary world and the solutions proposed. John Rawls, for example, in *A Theory of Justice* (Cambridge: Harvard University Press, Belknap Press, 1971), presupposes that the dominant tradition in modern society is liberal individualism based on the social contract as found in Locke, Rousseau, and Kant, a truncated view of the past that uses selected thinkers to characterize by implication broad social practice. Rawls's argument is based on an ahistorical rationalism, clinched at crucial points by such irrationalities as "our intuitive conviction" (p. 4), "it

seems natural to think" (p. 5), "principles that free and rational persons . . . would accept" (p. 11), "chosen by rational persons" (p. 16), "natural and plausible" (p. 18), "seems reasonable to suppose" (p. 19), etc. Even this dubiously grounded rationality seems caught in an unevenness, probably a contradiction, between a pragmatic conception of rationality as "the most effective means to a given end" (p. 14) and rationality as coherence (e.g., pp. 21 and 579). Alasdair MacIntyre, another example, in *After Virtue: A Study in Moral Theory* (Notre Dame, Ind.: University of Notre Dame Press, 1981), would have us believe that we live in a world in which "we have—very largely, if not entirely—lost our comprehension, both theoretical and practical, of morality" (p. 2); that there was once a consensus in Western society based on Aristotelianism, "*philosophically* the most powerful of pre-modern modes of moral thought" (p. 111); that this "lost morality" has been displaced by "emotivism," which rejects any "rational justification for an objective morality," and has led to a decline into fragmented morality; and that the choice must be made today between Aristotle and Nietzsche (chs. 9 and 18). The highly communal federal tradition, which characterizes so pervasively the practice of modern societies, appears to be unknown to Rawls and Mac-Intyre. Their knowledge of Western history is deficient and distorted. As a result, their alarms, analyses, and solutions seem largely irrelevant to the realities of the world they are supposedly addressing.

3. Blakey, *The History of Political Literature*, 2:347.

4. Von Gierke, *The Development of Political Theory*, p. 266.

5. Von Gierke, *Natural Law and the Theory of Society, 1500 to 1800*, p. 70.

6. Sabine, *A History of Political Theory*, pp. 378–384, 416–420.

7. Ludwig Gumplowicz, *Geschichte der Staatstheorien* (Berlin, 1926), pp. 182–187.

8. Skinner, *The Foundations of Modern Political Thought*, 2:236.

9. Ibid., 2:235–331.

10. Ibid., 2:341, 350.

11. Schrenk, *Gottesreich und Bund*, p. 69.

12. There is still some question about Mornay's authorship, though the probability that he wrote the *Vindiciae* alone or with a limited amount of collaboration is regarded as high. See Franklin, *Constitutionalism and Resistance*.

13. Ibid., p. 143.

14. Ibid., pp. 144–145. See also Laski, *A Defense of Liberty Against Tyrants*, pp. 71–75, 80–85.

15. Laski, *A Defense of Liberty Against Tyrants*, pp. 87–116; and Franklin, *Constitutionalism and Resistance*, pp. 146–158.

16. Franklin, *Constitutionalism and Resistance*, p. 157.

17. Ibid., p. 158.

18. Ibid., pp. 158–179; and Laski, *A Defense of Liberty Against Tyrants,* pp. 117–174.

19. Franklin, *Constitutionalism and Resistance,* pp. 180–197; and Laski, *A Defense of Liberty Against Tyrants,* pp. 174–213.

20. Friedrich, *Trends of Federalism,* p. 14.

21. Friedrich, *Politica,* Introduction, p. xv. See also Carney, *Politics;* and McCoy, "The Centrality of Covenant in the Political Philosophy of Johannes Althusius."

22. See Carney, *Politics,* p. xv; Friedrich, *Politica,* p. xxiv.

23. Peter Ramus (1515–1572), a French philosopher, developed a method of thought that was, in its time, a strong alternative to Aristotelian scholasticism. His influence was felt especially, not only in Paris, where he taught, but also in Basel and Herborn and among Reformed thinkers generally. Ramus sought to recover the dialectical method of Plato, whose dialogues had for the first time become available in Europe in 1490, and replace the deductive method of scholasticism with the combination of induction from sensory experience within a continuous shaping of the organizing principles for categorizing and interpreting found in Plato's work. He became widely known early in his career for his master's thesis "Whatever Aristotle Has Said Is a Fabrication," meaning a fabrication of medieval scholastics. He also taught that "the starting point of all human knowledge of whatever kind is the sensuous experience and the induction from single instances" (*Dialecticae* [Frankfurt, 1610], p. 759; quoted in Friedrich, *Politica,* p. lxi). Ramus played an important role in shaping biblical interpretation, in the emergence of modern science, and in bringing Plato's thought back into use. His emphasis on method, on the natural functioning of the human mind, and on reasoning as very practical rather than abstract contributed also to the philosophy of Descartes. Ramus, a Protestant Christian, was strenuously opposed by Roman Catholic thinkers in Paris. He was assassinated in the massive slaughter of Protestants by Roman Catholics in the St. Bartholomew's Day Massacre in August 1572.

24. Friedrich, *Politica,* pp. xxvii–xxix.

25. Ibid., pp. xxxv–xli.

26. Von Gierke, *Althusius,* p. 226.

27. Friedrich, *Politica,* p. xxviii. See also pp. xlvii–lii for details on Althusius's use of the Bible and the places most frequently cited from it.

28. Ibid., pp. liif. and pp. lxviiif.

29. Carney, *Politics,* Preface by Carl J. Friedrich, p. viii.

30. Friedrich, *Politica,* pp. liii–lvi.

31. Ibid., pp. lvi–lx.

32. Carney, *Politics,* p. ix.

33. See Friedrich, *Politica*, pp. lxiiiff.
34. From Carney, *Politics*, p. 22.
35. Friedrich, *Politica*, p. lxvii.
36. Von Gierke, *Althusius*, p. 157.
37. Carney, *Politics*, pp. 4–5.
38. Ibid., p. 10.
39. See Hannah Arendt, *On Revolution* (New York: Viking Press, 1963). See also Charles S. McCoy, *When Gods Change: Hope for Theology* (Nashville: Abingdon Press, 1980), pp. 231ff.

Chapter 4: The Zenith of Federal Theology: Johannes Cocceius

1. Friedrich, *Politica*, p. xxviii.
2. J. F. Iken, "Matthias Martinus," *The New Schaff-Herzog Encyclopedia of Religious Knowledge* (New York, 1909), 7:217. (hereafter cited as *New S-H*).
3. Heppe, *Geschichte des Pietismus*, p. 212.
4. Martini was a prolific writer in the fields of sacred philology, dogmatics, exegesis, and polemics. His chief works were *Christianae doctrinae summa capita* (Herborn in Nassau, 1603); and *Lexicon philologico-etymologicum* (Bremen, 1623).
5. See H. C. Rogge, "Remonstrants," *New S-H*, 9:482.
6. See John Lothrop Motley, *The Life and Death of John of Barneveld*. 2 vols. (New York, 1874), for a detailed account of the intertwining of theological, political, and economic tensions in the period surrounding the Synod of Dort. The quotations from Prince Maurice appear in vol. 2, p. 57.
7. See ibid., 2:48–54, 94–101; and Thomas C. Grattan, *Holland: The History of the Netherlands* (New York, 1901), pp. 256–259.
8. See Ditchfield, *The Church in the Netherlands*, p. 280; Good, *History of the Swiss Reformed Church Since the Reformation*, p. 35; Schrenk, *Gottesreich und Bund*, p. 3; and Heppe, *Dogmatik des deutschen Protestantismus*, 1:156.
9. Barnouw, *The Pageant of Netherlands History*, p. 150.
10. Norman H. Snaith, "The Language of the Old Testament," *The Interpreter's Bible*, 12 vols. (New York and Nashville: Abingdon Press, 1951–1957), 1:229.
11. Schrenk, *Gottesreich und Bund*, p. vii.
12. Iken, "Die Brüder Gerhard und Johannes Coch," 3:200.
13. Schrenk, *Gottesreich und Bund*, p. 3.
14. Johannes Cocceius, *Summa doctrinae de foedere et testamento Dei*, ch. V, pars. 88–89 (hereafter cited as *Foed*), in *Opera Omnia*, 2nd ed., 8 vols. folio (Frankfurt-am-Main, 1689), vol. 7. Cocceius also discusses these points elsewhere.

15. Cocceius, *Aphorismi per universam theologiam breviores,* XIV, 13, in *Opera Omnia,* vol. 7 (hereafter cited as *Aph. brev.*).

16. Cocceius, *Foed.,* IV; also see Cocceius, *Summa theologiae ex scripturis repetita,* XLI; and idem, *Aphorismi per universam theologiam prolixiores,* V, 26, in *Opera Omnia,* vol. 7. (These latter two treatises will be referred to hereafter, respectively, as *ST* and *Aph. prol.*)

17. See esp. the Prefaces to *Foed.* and *ST.* See also *Aph. prol.,* II, 1–8.

18. Müller, "Johannes Cocceius and His School," 3:149. See also Heppe, *Geschichte des Pietismus,* pp. 219–220.

19. Cocceius, *ST,* I, 1. Karl Barth quotes this definition of theology by Cocceius at the beginning of his *Church Dogmatics,* vol. I/1, p. 1.

20. Cocceius, *Aph. brev.,* I, 20.

21. Dorner, *History of Protestant Theology,* 2:42.

22. Cocceius, *Commentarius in epistolam Pauli ad Romanos,* Preface, XXXV, in *Opera Omnia,* vol. 5.

23. Cocceius, *Aph. brev.,* III, 9.

24. Cocceius, *Aph. prol.,* II, 20.

25. Cocceius, *ST,* I, 4.

26. Cocceius, *Aph. prol.,* III, 13.

27. Cocceius, *Cogitationes de apocalypsi S. Johannis theologi,* XI, 9, in *Opera Omnia,* vol. 6.

28. Cocceius, *ST,* Preface.

29. Samuel Terrien, "History of the Interpretation of the Bible. III. Modern Period," *The Interpreter's Bible,* 1:128.

30. Cocceius, *Foed.,* IV and V; *ST,* XXLI; and elsewhere.

31. Cocceius, *Foed.,* I, 1. See Moltmann, "Geschichtstheologie und pietistisches Menschenbild bei Johann Coccejus und Theodor Undereyck."

Chapter 5: Federalism and the U.S. Constitution of 1787

1. William E. Gladstone, "Kin Beyond the Sea," *The North American Review* 127 (September 1878): 185.

2. William Bradford, *The History of Plymouth Plantation,* excerpts in *Colonial American Writing,* edited by Roy Harvey Pearce (New York: Rinehart, 1950), p. 34.

3. Ibid., pp. 34–35.

4. John Winthrop, "A Model of Christian Charity," in Miller, *American Puritans,* p. 82.

5. John Winthrop, "Speech to the General Court," in Miller, *American Puritans,* pp. 91–92.

6. John Cotton, "Limitation of Government," in Miller, *American Puritans,* p. 86.

7. John Cotton, "Letter to Lord Say and Seale, 1636," in *The Puritans*, edited by Perry Miller and Thomas H. Johnson (New York: American Book Co., 1938), pp. 209–211.

8. Lutz, "From Covenant to Constitution in American Political Thought," p. 101. The quotation Lutz uses is from Gordon Lloyd, "Textbooks in American Political Theory," *The Political Science Reviewer* 5 (Fall 1975): 314.

9. Henry Steele Commager, ed., *Documents of American History*, 4th ed. (New York: Appleton-Century-Crofts, 1948), p. 100.

10. Morey, "The Sources of American Federalism," p. 197.

11. Hobbes, *Leviathan; or, The Matter, Forme and Power of a Commonwealth Ecclesiasticall and Civil*, edited and with an Introduction by Michael Oakeshott. The Introduction by Oakeshott is superb and is helpful in overcoming some of the misunderstandings of Hobbes's thought. See also R. S. Peters, "Hobbes, Thomas," *The Encyclopedia of Philosophy*, 4:30–46, for an account of Hobbes's life and thought, and for a bibliography.

12. Hobbes, *Leviathan*, p. 5.

13. Peter Laslett, ed., *John Locke: Two Treatises of Government* (Cambridge: Cambridge University Press, 1966), p. 135.

14. See James Gordon Clapp, "Locke, John," *The Encyclopedia of Philosophy*, 4:487–503; and Richard I. Aaron, *John Locke*, 2d ed. (Oxford: Clarendon Press, 1955).

15. See D. G. C. MacNabb, "Hume, David," *The Encyclopedia of Philosophy*, 4:74–90.

16. Garry Wills, *Explaining America: The Federalist* (Garden City, N.Y.: Doubleday & Co., 1981).

17. Louis Hartz, *The Liberal Tradition in America: An Interpretation of American Political Thought Since the Revolution* (New York: Harcourt, Brace & Co., 1955), pp. 140 and 116.

18. Carl Van Doren, *The Great Rehearsal: The Story of the Making and Ratifying of the Constitution of the United States* (New York: Viking Press, 1948), p. 70.

19. Quoted in Martha Lou Lemmon Stohlman, *John Witherspoon: Parson, Politician, Patriot* (Philadelphia: Westminster Press, 1976), p. 15.

20. Witherspoon, "Lectures on Divinity," *Works* 8:88, 119–121.

21. Witherspoon, "Lectures on Moral Philosophy," *Works* 7:13, 101, 106.

22. Hamilton, Madison, and Jay, *The Federalist Papers* (New York: Bantam Books, 1982).

23. Speech of June 26, 1787, to the Constitutional Convention. Quoted in Paul Eidelberg, *The Philosophy of the American Constitution: A Reinterpretation of the Intentions of the Founding Fathers* (New York: Free Press, 1968), p. 143.

Bibliography
of Federal Theology
and Political Philosophy

Adam, Gottfried. *Der Streit um Prädestination im ausgehenden 16. Jahr-hundert: Eine Untersuchung zu den Entwürfen von Samuel Huber und Aegidius Hunnius.* Beiträge zur Geschichte und Lehre der refor-mierten Kirche 30. Neukirchen-Vluyn: Neukirchener Verlag, 1970.

Ahlstrom, Sydney E. "The Puritan Ethic and the Spirit of American Democracy." In *Calvinism and the Political Order,* edited by George L. Hunt, ch. 5. Philadelphia: Westminster Press, 1965.

Albright, William F. "The Hebrew Expression for 'Making a Cove-nant' in Pre-Israelite Documents." *Bulletin of the American Schools of Oriental Research* 121 (February 1951): 21–22.

Althaus, Paul. *Die Prinzipien der deutschen reformierten Dogmatik im Zeitalter der aristotelischen Scholastik.* Leipzig: Deichert, 1914. Re-print. Darmstadt, 1967.

Alves, Colin. *The Covenant: An Old Testament Course.* Cambridge: Cambridge University Press, 1957.

Armstrong, Brian G. *Calvinism and the Amyraut Heresy: Protestant Scholasticism and Humanism in Seventeenth-Century France.* Madison, Wisc.: University of Wisconsin Press, 1969.

Auer, F. "Das Alte Testament in der Sicht des Bundesgedankens." In *Lextua Veritas Festschrift,* pp. 1–15. Trier: H. Junmer, 1961.

Baab, Otto J. *The Theology of the Old Testament.* New York: Abingdon-Cokesbury Press, 1949.

Baker, J. Wayne. "Church, State, and Dissent: The Crisis of the Swiss Reformation, 1531–1536," *Church History* 57 (1988): 135–152.

———. *Covenant and Community in the Thought of Heinrich Bullinger.* Philadelphia: Center for the Study of Federalism, Temple Univer-sity, 1980.

———. "Covenant and Society: The Respublica Christiana in the Thought of Heinrich Bullinger." Diss., University of Iowa, 1970.

————. "Das Datum von Bullingers 'Antwort an Johannes Burchard.' "
  Zwingliana 14 (1976): 274–275.

————. *Heinrich Bullinger and the Covenant: The Other Reformed Tradition.* Athens, Ohio: Ohio University Press, 1980.

————. "In Defense of Magisterial Discipline: Bullinger's 'Tractatus de Excommunicatione' of 1568." In *Heinrich Bullinger, 1504–1575. Gesammelte Aufsätze zum 400. Todestag,* edited by Ulrich Gäbler and Erland Herkenrath, 1:141–159. Zurich: Theologischer Verlag, 1975.

Baltzer, Klaus. *The Covenant Formulary in Old Testament, Jewish and Early Christian Writings.* Translated by David E. Green. Oxford: Basil Blackwell Publisher, 1971.

Bangs, Carl O. *Arminius: A Study in the Dutch Reformation.* Nashville: Abingdon Press, 1971.

Barker, Ernest, ed. *Social Contract: Essays by Locke, Hume and Rousseau.* New York: Oxford University Press, 1948.

Barnouw, Adriaan J. *The Pageant of Netherlands History.* New York: Longmans, Green & Company, 1952.

Baron, Hans. "Calvinist Republicanism and Its Historical Roots." *Church History* 8 (1939): 30–42.

Barr, James. *The Scottish Covenanters.* 2nd ed. Glasgow: J. Smith, 1947.

Barth, Karl. *Church Dogmatics.* Edited by G. W. Bromiley and T. F. Torrance. Edinburgh: T. & T. Clark, 1949ff. Especially vols. I/1, II/2, III, and IV/1.

Battis, Emery. *Saints and Sectaries: Anne Hutchinson and the Antinomian Controversy in the Massachusetts Bay Colony.* Chapel Hill, N.C.: University of North Carolina Press, 1962.

Beach, George. "Covenantal Ethics." In *The Life of Choice: Some Liberal Religious Perspectives on Morality,* edited by Clark Kucheman. Boston: Beacon Press, 1978.

Beckwith, Roger T. "The Unity and Diversity of God's Covenants." *Tyndale Bulletin* 38 (1987): 93–118.

Beebe, David Lewis. "The Seals of the Covenant: The Doctrine and Place of the Sacraments and Censures in the New England Puritan Theology Underlying the Cambridge Platform of 1648." Diss. Pacific School of Religion, 1966.

Begrich, Joachim. "Berit: Ein Beitrag zur Erfassung einer alttestamentlichen Denkform." *Zeitschrift für die alttestamentliche Wissenschaft* 60 (1944): 1–11.

Bellah, Robert N. *The Broken Covenant: American Civil Religion in Time of Trial.* New York: Seabury Press, 1975.

Berg, Hans Georg vom. "Noch Einmal: Zur Datierung von Heinrich Bullingers 'Antwort an Johannes Burchard.' " *Zwingliana* 14 (1978): 581–589.

Biéler, André. *La pensée économique et sociale de Calvin.* Geneva: Librairie de l'Université, 1959.

Bierma, Lyle D. "Covenant or Covenants in the Theology of Olevianus." *Calvin Theological Journal* 22 (1987): 228–250.

———. "Federal Theology in the 16th Century: Two Traditions?" *Westminster Theological Journal* 45 (1983): 304–321.

———. *German Calvinism in the Confessional Age: The Covenant Theology of Caspar Olevianus.* Studies in Historical Theology 4. Durham, N.C.: Labyrinth Press, 1991.

———. "The Role of Covenant Theology in Early Reformed Orthodoxy." *Sixteenth Century Journal* 21, no. 3 (1990): 453–462.

Bizer, Ernst. *Studien zur Geschichte des Abendsmahlsstreits im 16. Jahrhundert.* 1940. Reprint. Darmstadt: Wissenschaftliche Buchgesellschaft, 1972.

Blakey, Robert. *The History of Political Literature, from the Earliest Times.* 2 vols. London: R. Bentley, 1855.

Blanke, Fritz. *Der junge Bullinger 1504–1531.* Zurich: Zwingli Verlag, 1942.

Blanke, Fritz, and Immanuel Leuschner. *Heinrich Bullinger: Vater der reformierten Kirche.* Zurich: Theologischer Verlag, 1990.

Blodgett, John T. "The Political Theory of the Mayflower Compact." *Publications of the Colonial Society of Massachusetts* 12 (1908–1909): 204–213.

Bogue, Carl W. "Jonathan Edwards and the Covenant of Grace." Diss., Free University of Amsterdam, 1975.

———. "Jonathan Edwards on the Covenant of Grace." In *Soli Deo Gloria: Essays in Reformed Theology,* edited by R. C. Sproul, pp. 134–145. Nutley, N.J.: Presbyterian and Reformed Publishing Co., 1976.

Bohatec, Josef. *Budé und Calvin: Studien zur Gedankenwelt des französischen Frühhumanismus.* Graz: Verlag Hermann Böhlaus, 1950.

———. "Die Methode der reformierten Dogmatik." *Theologische Studien und Kritiken* 81 (1908): 272–302.

Borowitz, Eugene B. "Covenant Theology—Another Look." *Worldview* 16 (March 1973): 21–27.

Bos, F. L. "[Piscator's] Beitrag zur Weiterführung der Bundestheologie." In *Johann Piscator: Ein Beitrag zur Geschichte der reformierten Theologie,* pp. 223–230. Kampen: J. H. Kok, 1932.

Bouvier, André. *Henri Bullinger réformateur et conseilleur oecuménique, le successeur de Zwingli, d'après sa correspondance avec les réformes et les humanistes de langue française.* Neuchâtel: Delachaux & Niestlé, 1940.

Breen, T. H. *The Character of the Good Ruler: Puritan Political Ideas in New England, 1630–1730.* New Haven: Yale University Press, 1970.

———. "English Origins and New World Development: The Case of Covenanted Militia in Seventeenth-Century Massachusetts." *Past and Present* 57 (1972): 74–96.

Breward, Ian. "The Life and Theology of William Perkins, 1558–
1602." Ph.D. diss., University of Manchester, 1963.
————, ed. *The Work of William Perkins*. Courtenay Library of Refor-
mation Classics 3. Appleford, Abingdon, England: Sutton Courte-
nay Press, 1970.
Bright, John. *Covenant and Promise: The Prophetic Understanding of the
Future in Pre-Exilic Israel*. Philadelphia: Westminster Press, 1976.
Brown, W. Adams. "Covenant Theology." *Encyclopedia of Religion and
Ethics*, edited by James Hastings, 4: 216–224.
Buber, Martin. *Moses: The Revelation and the Covenant*. New York:
Harper & Brothers, 1959.
Buchanan, George Wesley. *The Consequences of the Covenant*. Leiden:
E. J. Brill, 1970.
Burrage, Champlin. *The Church Covenant Idea: Its Origin and Its
Development*. Philadelphia: American Baptist Publication Society,
1904.
Burrell, Sidney A. "The Apocalyptic Vision of the Early Covenan-
ters." *Scottish Historical Review* 43 (1964): 1–24.
————. "The Covenant Idea as a Revolutionary Symbol: Scotland
1596–1637." *Church History* 27 (1958): 338–350.
Busch, Eberhard. "Der Beitrag und Ertrag der Föderaltheologie für
ein geschichtliches Verständnis der Offenbarung." In *Oikonomia:
Heilsgeschichte als Thema der Theologie. Festschrift für Oscar Cullmann*,
edited by Felix Christ, pp. 171–190. Hamburg-Bergstadt: Reich,
1967.
Buss, Martin J. "The Covenant Theme in Historical Perspective."
Vetus Testamentum 16 (1966): 502–504.
Büsser, Fritz. *Würzeln der Reformation in Zürich*. Studies in Medieval
and Reformation Thought 31. Leiden: E. J. Brill, 1985.
Butler, Charles J. *Covenant Theology and the Development of Religious
Liberty*. Philadelphia: Center for the Study of Federalism, Temple
University, 1980.
Calvin, John. *Institutes of the Christian Religion*. Edited by John T.
McNeill; translated by Ford Lewis Battles. 2 vols. Library of Chris-
tian Classics. Philadelphia: Westminster Press, 1960.
Cameron, James K. "The Swiss and the Covenant." In *The Scottish
Tradition*, edited by G. W. S. Barrow. Edinburgh: Scottish Academic
Press, 1974.
Campbell, Douglas. *The Puritan in Holland, England, and America: An
Introduction to American History*. 4th ed. 2 vols. New York: Harper &
Brothers, 1893.
Carden, Allen. "The Communal Ideal in Puritan New England,
1630–1700." *Fides et Historia*, 17, no. 1 (Fall 1984): 25–38.
Carney, Frederick, ed. and trans. *The Politics of Johannes Althusius*. An
abridged translation of the 3rd ed. of *Politica Methodice Digesta*,

atque exemplis sacris et profanis illustrata, and including the Prefaces to the 1st and 3rd eds. Boston: Beacon Press, 1964.

Chalker, William H. "Calvin and Some Seventeenth Century English Calvinists." Diss., Duke University, 1961.

Cherry, C. Conrad. "Covenant Relation." In *The Theology of Jonathan Edwards: A Reappraisal,* pp. 107–123. Garden City, N.Y.: Doubleday & Co., Anchor Books, 1966.

————. "The Puritan Notion of the Covenant in Jonathan Edwards' Doctrine of Faith." *Church History* 34 (1965): 328–341.

Christy, Wayne Herron. "John Cotton: Covenant Theologian." Master of Arts thesis, Pittsburgh-Xenia Theological Seminary, 1942.

Clebsch, William A. *England's Earliest Protestants 1520–1535.* New Haven, Conn.: Yale University Press, 1964.

Clouse, Robert G. "Covenant Theology." *The New International Dictionary of the Christian Church* (1974), p. 267.

Coenen, Lothar. "Gottes Bund und Erwählung." In *Handbuch zum Heidelberger Katechismus,* edited by Lothar Coenen, pp. 126–135. Neukirchen-Vluyn: Neukirchener Verlag, 1963.

Collinson, Patrick. *The Elizabethan Puritan Movement.* London: Jonathan Cape, 1967.

Coolidge, John S. *The Pauline Renaissance in England: Puritanism and the Bible.* Oxford: Clarendon Press, 1970.

Cottrell, Jack Warren. "Covenant and Baptism in the Theology of Huldreich Zwingli." Diss., Princeton Theological Seminary, 1971.

————. "Is Bullinger the Source of Zwingli's Doctrine of the Covenant?" In *Heinrich Bullinger, 1504–1575. Gesammelte Aufsätze zum 400. Todestag,* edited by Ulrich Gäbler and Erland Herkenrath, 1:75–83. Zurich: Theologischer Verlag, 1975.

Courtenay, William J. *Covenant and Causality in Medieval Thought: Studies in Philosophy, Theology, and Economic Practice.* London: Variorum Reprints, 1984.

Courvoisier, Jacques. *La notion d'église chez Bucer dans son développement historique.* Paris: Librairie Felix Alcan, 1933.

"Covenant Theology." (n.a.) *The Westminster Dictionary of Church History* (1971), p. 243.

Cowan, Ian B. *The Scottish Covenanters: 1600–1688.* London: Victor Gollancz, 1976.

Currie, Mary M. "The Puritan Half-Way Covenants: A Contemporary Issue." *Austin Seminary Bulletin* 95 (1979): 29–39.

Daniel, E. Randolph. "Reconciliation, Covenant and Election: A Study in the Theology of John Donne." *Anglican Theological Review* 48 (1966): 14–30.

Davidson, Edward H. "The Covenant and God's Incentives." In *Jonathan Edwards: The Narrative of a Puritan Mind,* pp. 37–56. Boston: Houghton Mifflin Co., 1966.

De Jong, Peter Y. *The Covenant Idea in New England Theology, 1620–1847*. Grand Rapids: Wm. B. Eerdmans Publishing Co., 1945.

Dickens, A. G. *The English Reformation*. New York: Schocken Books, 1964.

Diemer, N. *Het scheppingsverbond met Adam (het verbond der werken), bij de theologen der 16e, 17e en 18e eeuw in Zwitserland, Duitschland, Nederland en Engeland*. Kampen: J. H. Kok, 1935.

Diestel, Ludwig. *Geschichte des Alten Testamentes in der christlichen Kirche*. Jena: Mauke's Verlag, 1869.

————. "Studien zur Föderaltheologie." *Jahrbuch für deutsche Theologie* 10 (1865): 209–276.

Dillistone, Frederick W. *The Structure of the Divine Society*. Philadelphia: Westminster Press, 1951.

Ditchfield, Peter Hampson. *The Church in the Netherlands*. London: Wells Gardner, Darton & Co., 1893.

Dorner, Isaak August. *History of Protestant Theology, Particularly in Germany*. 2 vols. Translated by George Robson and Sophia Taylor. Edinburgh: T. & T. Clark, 1871.

Dow, Norman. "A Select Bibliography on the Concept of Covenant." *Austin Seminary Bulletin* 78 (1963): 52–62.

Dowey, Edward A., Jr. "Der theologische Aufbau des Zweiten Helvetischen Bekenntnisses." In *Glauben und Bekennen: Vierhundert Jahre Confessio Helvetica Posterior: Beiträge zu ihrer Geschichte und Theologie*, edited by Joachim Staedtke, pp. 205–234. Zurich: Zwingli Verlag, 1966.

Ebrard, Johannes Heinrich August. "Cocceius, Johannes." *A Religious Encyclopaedia or Dictionary of Biblical, Historical, Doctrinal and Practical Theology*. 2nd ed. Vol. 1 (1891), pp. 503–504.

————. "Cocceius und seine Schule." *Realencyklopädie für protestantische Theologie und Kirche*. 2nd ed. Vol. 3 (1878), pp. 291–296.

Eichrodt, Walther. *Theology of the Old Testament*. Translated by J. A. Baker. Philadelphia: Westminster Press, 1967.

Elazar, Daniel J. *Exploring Federalism*. Tuscaloosa: University of Alabama Press, 1987.

————. *From Biblical Covenant to Modern Federalism: The Federal Theology Bridge*. Philadelphia: Center for the Study of Federalism, Temple University, 1980.

————. "The Political Theory of Covenant: Biblical Origins and Modern Developments." *Publius* 10, no. 4 (1980): 3–30.

Elazar, Daniel J., and John Kincaid, eds. "Covenant, Polity and Constitutionalism." *Publius* 10, no. 4 (1980).

Emerson, Everett H. "Calvin and Covenant Theology." *Church History* 25 (1956): 136–144.

Eusden, John Dykstra. *The Marrow of Theology: William Ames 1576–1633*. Boston: Pilgrim Press, 1968.

———. "Natural Law and Covenant Theology." *Natural Law Forum* 5 (1960): 1–30.

———. *Puritans, Lawyers, and Politics in Early Seventeenth-Century England.* New Haven: Yale University Press, 1958.

Evans, E. Lewis. "Bundestheologie." *Weltkirchenlexicon* (1960), pp. 196–198.

Everett, William Johnson. *God's Federal Republic: Reconstructing Our Governing Symbol.* New York: Paulist Press, 1988.

Farner, Alfred. *Die Lehre von Kirche und Staat bei Zwingli.* Tübingen: J. C. B. Mohr (Paul Siebeck), 1930.

Fast, Heinold. *Heinrich Bullinger und die Taufer: Ein Beitrag zur Historiographie und Theologie im 16. Jahrhundert.* Schriftenreihe des Mennonitischen Geschichtsverein, F. Weierhof (Pfalz): Mennonitischen Geschichtsverein, 1959.

Faulenbach, Heiner. "Coccejus, Johannes (1603–1669)." *Theologische Realenzyklopädie* 8 (1981): 132–140.

———. *Weg und Ziel der Erkenntnis Christi: Eine Untersuchung zur Theologie des Johannes Cocceius.* Beiträge zur Geschichte und Lehre der reformierten Kirche 36. Neukirchen-Vluyn: Neukirchener Verlag, 1973.

Ferguson, Sinclair B. "The Teaching of the Confession." In *The Westminster Confession in the Church Today,* edited by A. I. C. Heron, pp. 28–39. Edinburgh: Saint Andrew Press, 1982.

Fiering, Norman. *Jonathan Edwards's Moral Thought and Its British Context.* Chapel Hill, N.C.: University of North Carolina Press, 1981.

Fisch, Harold. *Covenant Motifs in Seventeenth Century English Literature.* Philadelphia: Center for the Study of Federalism, Temple University, 1980.

———. *Hamlet and the Word: The Covenant Pattern in Shakespeare.* New York: Ungar Publishing Co., 1971.

Fischer, Joseph. "Die Einheit der beiden Testamente bei Laktanz, Viktorin von Pettau und anderen Quellen." *Münchener theologische Zeitschrift* 1 (1950): 96–101.

Fisher, George Park. "The Augustinian and the Federal Theories of Original Sin Compared." *The New Englander* 27 (1868): 468–516.

———. "Scoto-Calvinism and Anglo-Puritanism: An Irenicum." *The British and Foreign Evangelical Review* 17 (1868): 255–275.

Forster, Winfried. "Thomas Hobbes und der Puritanismus: Grundlagen und Grundfragen seiner Staatslehre." *Beiträge zur politischen Wissenschaft,* vol. 8 (Berlin, 1969), pp. 74–126.

Foster, Herbert D. "The Political Theories of Calvinists Before the Puritan Exodus to America." *American Historical Review* 21 (1916): 481–503.

Franklin, Julian H. *Jean Bodin and the Rise of Absolutist Theory.* Cambridge: Cambridge University Press, 1973.

————, ed. and trans. *Constitutionalism and Resistance in the Sixteenth Century: Three Treatises by Hotman, Beza, and Mornay.* New York: Pegasus, 1969.

Freeman, Gordon. "The Rabbinic Understanding of Covenant as a Political Idea." Working Paper No. 2. Jerusalem and Philadelphia: Center for Jewish Community Studies, 1977.

Friedrich, Carl Joachim. *Politica Methodice Digesta of Johannes Althusius (Althaus).* Cambridge, Mass.: Harvard University Press, 1969.

————. *Trends of Federalism in Theory and Practice.* New York: Frederick A. Praeger, 1968.

Gäbler, Ulrich, and Erland Herkenrath, eds. *Heinrich Bullinger, 1504–1575. Gesammelte Aufsätze zum 400. Todestag.* 2 vols. Zürcher Beiträge zur Reformationsgeschichte 7, 8. Zurich: Theologischer Verlag, 1975.

Gardner, E. Clinton. "Justice in the Puritan Covenantal Tradition." In *The Annual of the Society of Christian Ethics,* edited by D. M. Yeager, pp. 91–111. Knoxville, Tenn.: Society of Christian Ethics, 1988.

Garrett, Christina Hollowell. *The Marian Exiles: A Study in the Origins of Elizabethan Puritanism.* Cambridge: Cambridge University Press, 1938.

Gass, Wilhelm. *Geschichte der protestantischen Dogmatik.* Vol. 2. Berlin: G. Reimer, 1857.

Gerstner, John H. "The Covenantal Frame of Reference." In *Steps to Salvation: The Evangelistic Message of Jonathan Edwards,* pp. 173–188. Philadelphia: Westminster Press, 1960.

Gewirth, Alan. *Marsilius of Padua: The Defender of Peace,* Vol. 1: *Marsilius of Padua and Medieval Political Philosophy.* New York: Columbia University Press, 1951.

Gierke, Otto von. *The Development of Political Theory.* New York: W. W. Norton & Co., 1939.

————. *Johannes Althusius und die Entwicklung der naturrechtlichen Staatstheorien.* 5th ed. Meisenheim am Glan: Scientia Aalen, 1958.

————. *Natural Law and the Theory of Society, 1500 to 1800.* Cambridge: Cambridge University Press, 1950.

————. *Political Theories of the Middle Age.* Translated by Frederic William Maitland. Cambridge: Cambridge University Press, 1958.

Gildrie, Richard P. *Salem, Massachusetts, 1626–1683: A Covenant Community.* Charlottesville, Va.: University Press of Virginia, 1975.

Goebel, Max. "Dr. Caspar Olevianus." *Mercersburg Review* 7 (1855): 294–306.

Good, James I. *History of the Swiss Reformed Church Since the Reformation.* Philadelphia: Publications and Sunday School Board of the Reformed Church in the U.S., 1913.

Gough, John W. *The Social Contract: A Critical Study of Its Development.* 2nd ed. Oxford: Clarendon Press, 1957.

Greaves, Richard L. "John Bunyan and Covenant Thought in the Seventeenth Century." *Church History* 36 (1967): 151–169.

————. "John Knox and the Covenant Tradition." *Journal of Ecclesiastical History* 24 (1973): 23–32.

————. "The Origins and Early Development of English Covenant Thought." *The Historian* 31 (1968): 21–35.

Greschat, Martin. "Der Bundesgedanke in der Theologie des späten Mittelalters." *Zeitschrift für Kirchengeschichte* 81 (1970): 44–63.

Hagen, Kenneth. "From Testament to Covenant in the Early Sixteenth Century." *Sixteenth Century Journal* 3, no. 1 (1972): 1–24.

————. *A Theology of Testament in the Young Luther: The Lectures on Hebrews.* Studies in Medieval and Reformation Thought 12. Leiden: E. J. Brill, 1974.

Hagenbach, Karl R. *Lehrbuch der Dogmengeschichte.* Vol. 2. Leipzig: Hirzel, 1841. There were various revised German and revised English editions of this work. The discussions of federal theology did not substantially change in any of them.

Hall, David D. "Understanding the Puritans." In *The State of American History,* edited by Herbert J. Bass, pp. 330–349. Chicago: Quadrangle Books, 1970.

Haller, William. "The Puritan Background of the First Amendment." In *The Constitution Reconsidered,* edited by Conyers Read, pp. 131–141. New York: Columbia University Press, 1938.

Hamilton, Alexander, James Madison, and John Jay. *The Federalist Papers.* With an introduction and commentary by Garry Wills. New York: Bantam Books, 1982.

Hamm, Berndt. *Promissio, pactum, ordinatio: Freiheit und Selbstbindung Gottes in der scholastischen Gnadenlehre.* Beiträge zur historischen Theologie 54. Tübingen: J. C. B. Mohr (Paul Siebeck), 1977.

Harrison, A. H. W. *The Beginnings of Arminianism to the Synod of Dort.* London: University of London Press, 1926.

Haskins, George Lee. *Law and Authority in Early Massachusetts.* New York: Macmillan Co., 1960.

Hastie, William. *The Theology of the Reformed Church in Its Fundamental Principles.* Edited by William Fulton. Edinburgh: T. & T. Clark, 1904.

Helm, Paul. "Calvin and the Covenant: Unity and Continuity." *Evangelical Quarterly* 55 (1983): 65–81.

Henderson, George D. "The Idea of the Covenant in Scotland." *Evangelical Quarterly* 27 (1955): 2–14.

————. *Religious Life in Seventeenth Century Scotland.* Cambridge: Cambridge University Press, 1937.

Heppe, Heinrich. *Dogmatik des deutschen Protestantismus im sechzehnten Jahrhundert.* 3 vols. Gotha: F. A. Perthes, 1857.

———. *Geschichte des Pietismus und der Mystik in der reformirten Kirche, namentlich der Niederlände.* Leiden: E. J. Brill, 1879.

———. *Reformed Dogmatics: Set Out and Illustrated from the Sources.* Edited by Ernst Bizer; translated by G. T. Thompson. London: George Allen & Unwin, 1950.

Hewison, James King. *The Covenanters.* 2 vols. Glasgow: John Smith & Son, 1908.

Hobbes, Thomas. *Leviathan; or, The Matter, Forme and Power of a Commonwealth Ecclesiasticall and Civil.* Edited and with an Introduction by Michael Oakeshott. New York: Macmillan & Co., 1947.

Hoekema, Anthony A. "Calvin's Doctrine of the Covenant of Grace." *Reformed Review* 15 (1962): 1–12.

———. "The Covenant of Grace in Calvin's Teaching." *Calvin Theological Journal* 2 (1967): 133–161.

Holifield, E. Brooks. *The Covenant Sealed: The Development of Puritan Sacramental Theology in Old and New England 1570–1720.* New Haven: Yale University Press, 1974.

Hollweg, Walter. *Heinrich Bullingers Hausbuch: Eine Untersuchung über die Anfänge der reformierten Predigtliteratur.* Beiträge zur Geschichte und Lehre der reformierten Kirche 8. Neukirchen-Vluyn: Neukirchener Verlag, 1956.

Höpfl, Harro, and Martyn P. Thompson. "The History of Contract as a Motif in Political Thought," *American Historical Review* 84 (1979): 919–945.

Hüglin, Thomas O. "Althusius, Federalism, and the Notion of the State." *Il Pensiero Politico* 13 (1980): 225–232.

———. *Covenant and Federalism in the Politics of Althusius.* Philadelphia: Center for the Study of Federalism, Temple University, 1980.

Iken, J. F. "Die Brüder Gerhard und Johannes Coch (Cocceius) in Bremen." *Zeitschrift der Gesellschaft für niedersächsische Kirchengeschichte,* 3:197–223. Braunschweig: Albert Limbach, 1898.

Jacobs, P. "Bund: IV. Föderaltheologie, dogmengeschichtlich." *Die Religion in Geschichte und Gegenwart.* 3rd ed. Vol. 1 (1957), pp. 1518–1520.

Jocz, Jakob. *The Covenant: A Theology of Human Destiny.* Grand Rapids: Wm. B. Eerdmans Publishing Co., 1968.

Johnson, James T. "The Covenant Idea and the Puritan View of Marriage." *Journal of the History of Ideas* 32 (1971): 107–118.

Jones, James W. *The Shattered Synthesis: New England Puritanism Before the Great Awakening.* New Haven: Yale University Press, 1973.

Karlberg, Mark Walter. "The Mosaic Covenant and the Concept of Works in Reformed Hermeneutics: A Historical-Critical Analysis,

With Particular Attention to Early Covenant Eschatology." Diss., Westminster Theological Seminary, 1980.

———. "Reformed Interpretation of the Mosaic Covenant." *Westminster Theological Journal* 43 (1980): 1–57.

Kendall, R. T. *Calvin and English Calvinism to 1649.* Oxford: Oxford University Press, 1979.

———. "The Puritan Modification of Calvin's Theology." In *John Calvin: His Influence in the Western World,* edited by W. Stanford Reid, pp. 199–214. Grand Rapids: Zondervan Publishing House, 1982.

Ketcham, Ralph L. "James Madison and the Nature of Man." *Journal of the History of Ideas* 19 (1958): 62–76.

Kincaid, John, compiler. *Working Bibliography on Covenant and Politics.* Rev. ed. Philadelphia: Center for the Study of Federalism, Temple University, 1980.

Kincaid, John, and Daniel Elazar, eds. *The Covenant Connection: The Biblical Origins of Modern Politics.* Durham, N.C.: North Carolina Academic Press, forthcoming.

Klassen, William. *Covenant and Community: The Life, Writings and Hermeneutics of Pilgrim Marpeck.* Grand Rapids: Wm. B. Eerdmans Publishing Co., 1968.

Knappen, Marshall M. *Tudor Puritanism: A Chapter in the History of Idealism.* Chicago: University of Chicago Press, 1939.

Koch, Ernst. "Paulusexegese und Bundestheologie: Bullingers Auslegung von Gal 3: 17–26." In *Histoire de l'exégèse au XVIe siècle,* edited by O. Fatio and Pierre Fraenkel, pp. 342–350. Geneva: Droz, 1978.

———. *Die Theologie der Confessio Helvetica Posterior.* Beiträge zur Geschichte und Lehre der reformierten Kirche 27. Neukirchen-Vluyn: Neukirchener Verlag, 1968.

Korff, Emanuel Graf von. *Die Anfänge der Föderaltheologie und ihre erste Ausgestaltung in Zurich und Holland.* Bonn: Emil Eisele, 1908.

Kraus, Hans-Joachim. *Geschichte der historisch-kritischen Erforschung des Alten Testaments.* 2nd ed. Neukirchen-Vluyn: Neukirchener Verlag, 1969.

Lane, Tony. "The Quest for the Historical Calvin." *Evangelical Quarterly* 55 (1983): 95–113.

Lang, August. *Der Evangelienkommentar Martin Butzers und die Grundzüge seiner Theologie.* Studien zur Geschichte der Theologie und der Kirche. Leipzig: Dieterich'sche Verlags-Buchhandlung, T. Weicher, 1900.

———. *Der Heidelberger Katechismus und vier verwandte Katechismen (Leo Jud's und Micron's kleine Katechismen, sowie die zwei Vorarbeiten Ursins).* Reprint. Darmstadt: Wissenschaftliche Buchgesellschaft, 1967.

Laski, Harold J., ed. *A Defense of Liberty Against Tyrants: A Translation of the Vindiciae contra tyrannos by Junius Brutus.* 1924. Reprint. New York: Burt Franklin, 1972.

Laughlin, Paul Alan. "The Brightness of Moses's Face: Law and Gospel, Covenant and Hermeneutics in the Theology of William Tyndale." Diss., Emory University, 1975.

Leith, John H. *Assembly at Westminster: Reformed Theology in the Making.* Richmond: John Knox Press, 1973.

Letham, Robert. "The Foedus Operum: Some Factors Accounting for Its Development." *Sixteenth Century Journal* 14 (1983): 457–467.

Lettinga, Cornelius. *Covenant Theology and the Transformation of Anglicanism.* Diss., Johns Hopkins University, 1987.

Lillback, Peter Alan. "The Binding of God: Calvin's Role in the Development of Covenant Theology." Diss., Westminster Theological Seminary, 1985.

————. "Ursinus' Development of the Covenant of Creation: A Debt to Melanchthon or Calvin?" *Westminster Journal of Theology* 43 (1981): 247–288.

Lindsay, T. M. "The Covenant Theology." *The British and Foreign Evangelical Review* 28 (1879): 521–538.

Locher, Gottfried W. *Huldrych Zwingli in neuer Sicht: Zehn Beiträge zur Theologie der Zürcher Reformation.* Zurich/Stuttgart: Zwingli Verlag, 1969.

————. *Die Theologie Huldrych Zwinglis im Lichte seiner Christologie,* part 1: *Die Gotteslehre.* Zurich: Zwingli Verlag, 1952.

————. "Zwingli's Thought: New Perspectives." *Studies in the History of Christian Thought* 25. Leiden: E. J. Brill, 1981.

Locke, John. *Two Treatises of Government.* Edited by Peter Laslett. New York: Cambridge University Press, 1963.

Lovin, Robin W. "Equality and Covenant Theology." *Journal of Law and Religion* 2 (1984): 241–262.

Lowrie, Ernest Benson. *The Shape of the Puritan Mind: The Thought of Samuel Willard.* New Haven: Yale University Press, 1974.

Lutz, Donald S. "From Covenant to Constitution in American Political Thought." *Publius* 10 (1980): 101–133.

Lyall, Francis. "Of Metaphors and Analogies: Legal Language and Covenant Theology." *Scottish Journal of Theology* 32, no. 1 (1979): 1–17.

McClelland, Joseph C. "Covenant Theology: A Re-evaluation." *Canadian Journal of Theology* 3 (1957): 182–188.

McCoy, Charles S. "The Centrality of Covenant in the Political Philosophy of Johannes Althusius." In *Politische Theorie des Johannes Althusius,* edited by Karl-Wilhelm Dahm et al. Berlin: Duncker & Humblot, 1988.

————. *The Covenant in America: Renewing Our Expectations.* Berkeley: Pacific School of Religion, 1976.

———. *The Covenant Theology of Johannes Cocceius*. Diss., Yale University, 1957; Ann Arbor: University Microfilms, 1965.

———. "The Federal Tradition of Theology and Political Ethics: Background for Understanding the U.S. Constitution and Society." In *The Annual of the Society of Christian Ethics, 1988*. Edited by D. M. Yeager. Washington, D.C.: Georgetown University Press, 1988.

———. *History, Humanity, and Federalism in the Theology and Ethics of Johannes Cocceius*. Philadelphia: Center for the Study of Federalism, Temple University, 1980.

———. "Johannes Cocceius: Federal Theologian." *Scottish Journal of Theology* 16 (1963): 352–370.

McGiffert, Michael. "American Puritan Studies in the 1960s." *William and Mary Quarterly* (3rd ser.) 27 (1970): 35–67.

———. "Covenant, Crown and Commons in Elizabethan Puritanism." *Journal of British Studies* 20 (1981): 32–52.

———. "From Moses to Adam: The Making of the Covenant of Works." *Sixteenth Century Journal* 19 (1988): 131–155.

———. "Grace and Works: The Rise and Division of Covenant Divinity in Elizabethan Puritanism." *Harvard Theological Review* 75 (1982): 463–502.

———. "The Problem of the Covenant in Puritan Thought: Peter Bulkeley's Gospel Covenant." *New England Historical and Genealogical Register* 130 (1976): 107–129.

———. "William Tyndale's Conception of Covenant." *Journal of Ecclesiastical History* 32 (1981): 167–184.

MacKenzie, J. Ross. "The Covenant Theology: A Review Article." *Journal of Presbyterian History* 44 (1966): 198–204.

McLaughlin, Andrew C. *Foundations of American Constitutionalism*. New York: New York University Press, 1932.

Marsden, George M. "Perry Miller's Rehabilitation of the Puritans: A Critique." *Church History* 39 (1970): 91–105.

Mendenhall, George E. "Covenant." *Encyclopaedia Britannica* (Chicago, 1974), 5:226–230.

———. "Covenant Forms in Israelite Tradition." *Biblical Archeologist* 17 (September 1954): 50–76.

———. *Law and Covenant in Israel and the Ancient Near East*. Pittsburgh: Biblical Colloquium, 1955.

Miller, Charles. "The Spread of Calvinism in Switzerland, Germany and France." In *The Rise and Development of Calvinism*, edited by John H. Bratt, pp. 27–62. Grand Rapids: Wm. B. Eerdmans Publishing Co., 1959.

Miller, Perry. *Errand Into the Wilderness*. New York: Harper & Row, 1964.

———. "From the Covenant to the Revival." In *Nature's Nation*. Cambridge: Harvard University Press, Belknap Press, 1967.

————. "The Half-Way Covenant." *New England Quarterly* 5 (1933): 676–715.

————. *The New England Mind: From Colony to Province.* Cambridge, Mass.: Belknap Press, 1953.

————. *The New England Mind: The Seventeenth Century.* New York: Macmillan Co., 1939.

————. *Orthodoxy in Massachusetts, 1630–1650.* Cambridge, Mass.: Harvard University Press, 1933.

————, ed. *The American Puritans.* Garden City, N.Y.: Doubleday & Co., 1946.

Mitchell, Alexander. "The Theology of the Reformed Church, With Special Reference to the Westminster Standards." In *Report of Proceedings of the Second General Council of the Presbyterian Alliance,* pp. 474–484. Philadelphia: Presbyterian Journal, 1880.

Moeller, Jens G. "The Beginnings of Puritan Covenant Theology." *Journal of Ecclesiastical History* 14 (1963): 46–67.

————. "Melanchthons naturretslaere og foderalteologiens gerningspagt." *Dansk teologisk tidsskrift* 24 (1961): 79–92.

Möller, Grete. "Föderalismus und Geschichtsbetrachtung im XVII. und XVIII. Jahrhundert." *Zeitschrift für Kirchengeschichte* 50 (1931): 393–440.

Moltmann, Jürgen. "Föderaltheologie." *Lexikon für Theologie und Kirche* 4:190–192. Freiburg: Verlag Herder, 1960.

————. "Geschichtstheologie und pietistisches Menschenbild bei Johann Coccejus und Theodor Undereyck." *Evangelische Theologie* 19 (1959).

————. "Prädestination und Heilsgeschichte bei Moyse Amyraut: Ein Beitrag zur Geschichte der reformierten Theologie zwischen Orthodoxie und Aufklärung." *Zeitschrift für Kirchengeschichte* 65 (1954): 270–303.

————. *Prädestination und Perseveranz: Geschichte und Bedeutung der reformierten Lehre "de perseverantia sanctorum."* Beiträge zur Geschichte und Lehre der reformierten Kirche 12. Neukirchen-Vluyn: Neukirchener Verlag, 1961.

Morey, William C. "The Sources of American Federalism." *Annals of the American Academy of Political and Social Science* 6 (September 1895): 197–226.

Morgan, Edmund S. "The Half-Way Covenant." In *Visible Saints: The History of a Puritan Idea.* New York: New York University Press, 1963.

————. *The Puritan Dilemma: The Story of John Winthrop.* Boston: Little, Brown & Co., 1958.

————. *Puritan Political Ideas 1558–1794.* Indianapolis: Bobbs-Merrill Co., 1965.

Morgan, John. *Godly Learning: Puritan Attitudes Towards Reason, Learn-*

ing and Education, 1560–1640. Cambridge: Cambridge University Press, 1986.

Mozley, J. F. *Coverdale and His Bibles*. London: Lutterworth Press, 1953.

Muilenburg, James. "The Form and Structure of the Covenantal Formulations," *Vetus Testamentum* 9 (1959): 347–365.

Müller, E. F. Karl. "Cocceius, Johannes, and His School." *The New Schaff-Herzog Encyclopedia of Religious Knowledge*, vol. 3 (1909), pp. 149–150.

Muller, Richard A. *Christ and the Decree: Christology and Predestination in Reformed Theology from Calvin to Perkins*. Studies in Historical Theology 2. Durham, N.C.: Labyrinth Press, 1986.

———. "Covenant and Conscience in English Reformed Theology: Three Variations on a 17th Century Theme." *Westminster Journal of Theology* 42 (1980): 308–334.

———. "The Federal Motif in Seventeenth Century Arminian Theology." *Nederlands Archief voor Kerkgeschiedenis* 62 (1982): 102–122.

———. "Predestination and Christology in Sixteenth Century Reformed Theology." Diss., Duke University, 1976.

———. "The Spirit and the Covenant: John Gill's Critique of the Pactum Salutis." *Foundations* 24 (1981): 4–14.

Munson, Charles Robert. "William Perkins: Theologian of Transition." Ph.D. diss., Case Western Reserve University, 1971.

Murray, John. *The Covenant of Grace: A Biblico-Theological Study*. London: Tyndale Press, 1954.

———. "Covenant Theology." *The Encyclopedia of Christianity*, vol. 3 (1972), pp. 199–216.

Nevin, J. W. "Zacharius Ursinus." *Mercersburg Review* 3 (1851): 490–512.

New, John F. H. *Anglican and Puritan: The Basis of Their Opposition, 1558–1640*. Stanford, Calif.: Stanford University Press, 1964.

Niebuhr, H. Richard. "The Idea of Covenant and American Democracy." *Church History* 23 (1954): 126–135.

———. *The Kingdom of God in America*. New York: Harper & Brothers, 1957.

———. "The Protestant Movement and Democracy in the United States." In *The Shaping of American Religion*, edited by James W. Smith and A. Leland Jamison, pp. 20–71. Princeton: Princeton University Press, 1961.

Niesel, Wilhelm. *The Theology of Calvin*. Translated by Harold Knight. London: Lutterworth Press, 1956.

Nordmann, Walter. "Im Widerstreit von Mystik und Föderalismus." *Zeitschrift für Kirchengeschichte* 50 (1931): 146–185.

Nuttall, Geoffrey F. *Visible Saints: The Congregational Way 1640–1660*. Oxford: Basil Blackwell, 1957.

Oakley, Francis. *Omnipotence, Covenant, and Order: An Excursion in the History of Ideas from Abelard to Leibniz.* Ithaca, N.Y.: Cornell University Press, 1984.

Oberman, Heiko A. *The Harvest of Medieval Theology: Gabriel Biel and Late Medieval Nominalism.* Grand Rapids: Wm. B. Eerdmans Publishing Co., 1967.

————. "The Shape of Late Medieval Thought: The Birthpangs of the Modern Era." In *The Pursuit of Holiness in Late Medieval and Renaissance Religion,* edited by Charles E. Trinkaus, pp. 3–25. Studies in Medieval and Reformation Thought 10. Leiden: E. J. Brill 1974.

————. "Wir sind pettler: Hoc est verum: Bund und Gnade in der Theologie des Mittelalters und der Reformation." *Zeitschrift für Kirchengeschichte* 78 (1967): 232–252.

Oestreich, Gerhard. "Die Idee des religiösen Bundes und die Lehre vom Staatsvertrag." In *Geist und Gestalt des frühmodernen Staates: Ausgewählte Aufsätze,* pp. 157–178. Berlin: Duncker & Humblot, 1969.

Osterhaven, M. Eugene. "Calvin on the Covenant." *Reformed Review* 33 (1980): 136–149.

Ostrom, Vincent. "Hobbes, Covenant and Constitution." *Publius* 10 (1980): 83–100.

Patry, Raoul. *Philippe du Plessis-Mornay: Un huguenot homme d'état.* Paris: Librairie Fischbacher, 1933.

Paul, Roberts S. "The Covenant in Church History." *Austin Seminary Bulletin* 96 (March 1981): 38–50.

Pedersen, Johannes. *Israel: Its Life and Culture.* 4 vols. London: Oxford University Press, 1926–1940.

Perlitt, Lothar. *Bundestheologie im Alten Testament.* Neukirchen-Vluyn: Neukirchener Verlag, 1969.

Perry, Ralph Barton. *Puritanism and Democracy.* New York: Vanguard Press, 1944.

Pestalozzi, Carl. *Heinrich Bullinger: Leben und ausgewählte Schriften. Nach handschriftlichen und gleichzeitigen Quellen.* Leben und ausgewählte Schriften der Väter und Begründer der reformirten Kirche. Elberfeld: R. L. Friderichs, 1858.

Peters, Ronald M. *The Massachusetts Constitution of 1780: A Social Compact.* Amherst: University of Massachusetts Press, 1978.

Pettit, Norman. *The Heart Prepared: Grace and Conversion in Puritan Spiritual Life.* New Haven: Yale University Press, 1966.

Pfister, Rudolf. *Kirchengeschichte der Schweiz,* vol. 2: *Von der Reformation bis zum Zweiten Villmerger Krieg.* Zurich: Theologischer Verlag, 1974.

Plumstead, A. W., ed. *The Wall and the Garden: Selected Massachusetts Election Sermons, 1670–1775.* Minneapolis: University of Minnesota Press, 1968.

Pollard, Alfred W., ed. *Records of the English Bible: The Documents Relating to the Translation and Publication of the Bible in English, 1525–1611.* Oxford: Oxford University Press, 1911.

Pope, Robert G. *The Half-Way Covenant: Church Membership in Puritan New England.* Princeton: Princeton University Press, 1969.

Potter, George R. *Zwingli.* Cambridge: Cambridge University Press, 1976.

Potter, Mary Lane. "The 'Whole Office of the Law' in the Theology of John Calvin." *Journal of Law and Religion* 3, no. 1 (1985): 117–139.

Preus, James Samuel. *From Shadow to Promise: Old Testament Interpretation from Augustine to Luther.* Cambridge: Harvard University Press, Belknap Press, 1969.

———. "Zwingli, Calvin and the Origin of Religion." *Church History* 46 (1977): 186–202.

Priebe, Victor Lewis. "The Covenant Theology of William Perkins." Diss., Drew University, 1967.

Reid, W. Stanford. "John Knox's Theology of Political Government." *Sixteenth-Century Journal* 19 (1988): 529–540.

Riley, Patrick. "Three 17th Century German Theorists of Federalism: Althusius, Hugo and Leibniz." *Publius* 6 (1976): 7–41.

Ritschl, Albrecht. *Geschichte des Pietismus.* 3 vols. Bonn: Adolph Marcus, 1880-1886.

Ritschl, Otto. *Dogmengeschichte des Protestantismus.* 4 vols. Göttingen: Vandenhoeck & Ruprecht, 1908–1927.

Robinson, Lewis Milton. "A History of the Half-Way Covenant." Ph.D. diss., University of Illinois, 1963.

Rogge, H. C. "Remonstrants." *The New Schaff-Herzog Encyclopedia of Religious Knowledge,* 9: 482.

Rolston, Holmes, III. *John Calvin Versus the Westminster Confession.* Richmond: John Knox Press, 1972.

Rossiter, Clinton. *Seedtime of the Republic.* New York: Harcourt, Brace & Co., 1953.

Rupp, E. Gordon. "Patterns of Salvation in the First Age of the Reformation." *Archiv für Reformationsgeschichte* 57 (1966): 52–66.

Ryrie, Charles C. *Dispensationalism Today.* Chicago: Moody Press, 1965.

Sabine, George H. *A History of Political Theory.* New York: Henry Holt & Co., 1938.

Salmon, J. H. M. *The French Religious Wars in English Political Thought.* Oxford: Clarendon Press, 1959.

Sargent, Mark L. "The Conservative Covenant: The Rise of the Mayflower Compact in American Myth." *New England Quarterly* 61 (1988): 233–251.

Schaff, Philip, ed. *The Creeds of Christendom.* 3 vols. 1877. Reprint. Grand Rapids: Baker Book House, 1977.

Scheel, Otto. "Föderaltheologie." *Die Religion in Geschichte und Gegenwart* (1st ed.), vol. 2 (1910), pp. 922–924.

Schneider, Herbert W. "The Puritan Tradition." In *Wellsprings of the American Spirit,* edited by F. Ernest Johnson, ch. 1. New York and London: Institute for Religious and Social Studies, 1948.

Schrenk, Gottlob. "Bund: III. Föderaltheologie, dogmengeschichtlich." *Die Religion in Geschichte und Gegenwart* (2nd ed.), vol. 1 (1927), pp. 1364–1367.

————. *Gottesreich und Bund im älteren Protestantismus, vornehmlich bei Johannes Cocceius.* Gütersloh: Bertelsmann, 1923.

Schulthess-Rechberg, Gustav von. *Heinrich Bullinger der Nachfolger Zwinglis.* Schriften des Vereins für Reformationsgeschichte 22. Halle: Verein für Reformationsgeschichte, 1904.

Schweizer, Alexander. *Die protestantischen Centraldogmen in ihrer Entwicklung innerhalb der reformirten Kirche.* 2 vols. Vol. 1, *Das 16. Jahrhundert.* Zurich: Orell, Fuessli, 1854–1856.

Scott, J. L. "The Covenant Theology of Karl Barth." *Scottish Journal of Theology* 17 (1964).

Seidman, Aaron B. "Church and State in the Early Years of Massachusetts Bay Colony." *New England Quarterly* 18 (1945): 211–233.

Sepp, Christiaan, *Het Godgeleerd Onderwijs in Nederland, gedurende de 16e en 17e Eeuw.* 2 vols. Leiden: De Breuk & Smits, 1873–1874.

Shaw, Mark Randolph. "The Marrow of Practical Divinity: A Study in the Theology of William Perkins." Diss., Westminster Theological Seminary, 1981.

Shipton, Clifford K. "Puritanism and Modern Democracy." *New England Historical and Genealogical Register* 101 (July 1947): 181–198.

Simon, Matthias. "Die Beziehung zwischen Altem und Neuem Testament in der Schriftauslegung Calvins." *Reformierte Kirchen Zeitung* 82 (1932), no. 3, 17–21; no. 4, 25–28; no. 5, 33–35.

Simpson, Alan. *Puritanism in Old and New England.* Chicago: University of Chicago Press, 1955.

Skinner, Quentin. *The Foundations of Modern Political Thought,* vol. 2: *The Age of Reformation.* Cambridge: Cambridge University Press, 1976.

Snaith, Norman H. *The Distinctive Ideas of the Old Testament.* London: Epworth Press, 1944.

Sommerville, C. J. "Conversion, Sacrament and Assurance in the Puritan Covenant of Grace, to 1650." Master of Arts thesis, University of Kansas, 1963.

————. "Conversion Versus the Early Puritan Covenant of Grace." *Journal of Presbyterian History* 44 (1966): 178–197.

Sprunger, Keith L. *The Learned Doctor William Ames: Dutch Backgrounds of English and American Puritanism.* Urbana, Ill.: University of Illinois Press, 1972.

Staedtke, Joachim. "Die Juden im historischen und theologischen Urteil des Schweizer Reformators Heinrich Bullinger." *Judaica* 11 (1955): 236–256.

———. *Die Theologie des jungen Bullinger.* Studien zur Dogmengeschichte und systematischen Theologie 16. Zurich: Zwingli Verlag, 1962.

———, ed. *Glauben und Bekennen: Vierhundert Jahre Confessio Helvetica Posterior: Beiträge zu ihrer Geschichte und Theologie.* Zurich: Zwingli Verlag, 1966.

Staehelin, Ernst. *Das theologische Lebenswerk Johannes Oekolampads.* Quellen und Forschungen zur Reformationsgeschichte 21. Leipzig: M. Heinsius, 1939.

Steinmetz, David C. "Heinrich Bullinger (1504–1575): Covenant and the Continuity of Salvation History." In *Reformers in the Wings,* edited by David C. Steinmetz, pp. 133–142. Philadelphia: Fortress Press, 1971.

Stoever, William Kenneth Bristow. "The Covenant of Works in Puritan Theology: The Antinomian Crisis in New England." Diss., Yale University, 1970.

———. *"A Faire and Easie Way to Heaven": Covenant Theology and Antinomianism in Early Massachusetts.* Middletown, Conn.: Wesleyan University Press, 1978.

———. "Nature, Grace and John Cotton: The Theological Dimension in the New England Antinomian Controversy." *Church History* 44 (1975): 22–34.

Stout, Harry S. "Word and Order in Colonial New England." In *The Bible in America: Essays in Cultural History,* edited by Nathan O. Hatch and Mark A. Noll, pp. 19–38. New York: Oxford University Press, 1982.

Strehle, Stephen. *Calvinism, Federalism, and Scholasticism: A Study of the Reformed Doctrine of the Covenant.* Basler und Berner Studien zur historischen und systematischen Theologie 58. Bern: Peter Lang, 1988.

Strout, Cushing. *The New Heavens and the New Earth: Political Religion in America.* New York: Harper & Row, 1976.

Sturm, Erdmann K. *Der junge Zacharias Ursin: Sein Weg vom Philippismus zum Calvinismus (1534–1562).* Beiträge zur Geschichte und Lehre der reformierten Kirche 33. Neukirchen-Vluyn: Neukirchener Verlag, 1972.

Sudhoff, Karl. *C. Olevianus und Z. Ursinus: Leben und ausgewählte Schriften.* Leben und ausgewählte Schriften der Vater und Begründer der reformirten Kirche 8. Elberfeld: R. L. Friderichs, 1857.

Tanis, James. *Dutch Calvinistic Pietism in the Middle Colonies: A Study in the Life and Theology of Theodorus Jacobus Freylinghuysen.* The Hague: Martinus Nijhoff, 1967.

Thompson, Bard, et al. *Essays on the Heidelberg Catechism*. Philadelphia and Boston: United Church Press, 1963.

Thundyl, Zacharias. *Covenant in Anglo-Saxon Thought*. Madras, India: The Macmillan Co. of India, 1972.

Toft, Daniel John. "Zacharias Ursinus: A Study in the Development of Calvinism." Master of Arts thesis, University of Wisconsin, 1962.

Toon, Peter. *The Emergence of Hyper-Calvinism in English Nonconformity, 1689–1765*. London: Olive Tree, 1967.

———. *God's Statesman: The Life and Work of John Owen*. Exeter, England: Paternoster Press, 1971.

Torok, Istvan. "Die Bewertung des Alten Testamentes in der Institution Calvins." In *Kálvin és a Kálvinizmus*, edited by Varga Zsigmond, pp. 121–139. Debrecen, Hungary, 1936.

Torrance, James B. "Calvinism and Puritanism in England and Scotland: Some Basic Concepts in the Development of 'Federal Theology.'" In *Calvinus Reformator*, pp. 264–286. Potchefstroom, South Africa, 1982.

———. "The Covenant Concept in Scottish Theology and Politics and Its Legacy." *Scottish Journal of Theology* 34 (1981): 225–243.

———. "Covenant or Contract? A Study of the Theological Background of Worship in Seventeenth-Century Scotland." *Scottish Journal of Theology* 23 (1970): 51–76.

———. "Strengths and Weaknesses of the Westminster Theology," In *The Westminster Confession in the Church Today*, edited by A. I. C. Heron, pp. 40–54. Edinburgh: Saint Andrew Press, 1982.

Trinterud, Leonard J. "The Origins of Puritanism." *Church History* 20 (1951): 37–57.

Usteri, Johann Martin. "Vertieferung der Zwinglischen Sakraments und Tauflehre bei Bullinger." *Theologische Studien und Kritiken* 1 (Gotha, 1883): 730–758.

Van den Bergh, Willem. *Calvijn over het Genade verbond*. The Hague, 1879.

Van Dyken, Seymour. *Samuel Willard: Preacher of Orthodoxy in an Era of Change*. Grand Rapids: Wm. B. Eerdmans Publishing Co., 1972.

Van t'Hooft, Antonius Johannes. *De theologie van Heinrich Bullinger in betrekking tot de Nederlandsche Reformatie*. Amsterdam: Is. de Hoogh, 1888.

Van Zandt, A. B. "The Doctrine of the Covenants Considered as the Central Principle of Theology." *Presbyterian Review* 3 (1882): 28–39.

Veninga, James Frank. "Covenant Theology and Ethics in the Thought of John Calvin and John Preston." Diss., Rice University, 1974.

Visser, Derk. "The Covenant in Zacharius Ursinus." *Sixteenth Century Journal* 18 (1987): 531–544.

Vitringa, Campegius. *Doctrina Christianae religionis per aphorismos summatim descripta*. 6th ed. Vol. 2. Leiden, 1776.

Von Rohr, John. "Covenant and Assurance in Early English Puritanism." *Church History* 34 (1965): 195–203.

———. *The Covenant of Grace in Puritan Thought.* Atlanta: Scholars Press, 1986.

Vos, Geerhardus. "The Doctrine of the Covenant in Reformed Theology." In *Redemptive History and Biblical Interpretation: The Shorter Writings of Geerhardus Vos,* edited by Richard B. Gaffin, pp. 234–267. Phillipsburg, N.J.: 1980.

Walker, George Leon. "Jonathan Edwards and the Half-Way Covenant." *The New Englander* 182 (1884): 601–614.

Walker, Williston. *The Creeds and Platforms of Congregationalism.* New York: Charles Scribner's Sons, 1893.

———. *A History of the Christian Church.* New York: Charles Scribner's Sons, 1926.

Wallace, Dewey D., Jr. *Puritans and Predestination: Grace in English Protestant Theology, 1525–1695.* Studies in Religion. Chapel Hill, N.C.: University of North Carolina Press, 1982.

Weinfeld, Moshe. "Covenant Terminology in the Ancient Near East and Its Influence on the West." *Journal of the American Oriental Society* 93 (1973): 190–199.

Weir, D. A. *The Origins of Federal Theology in Sixteenth-Century Reformation Thought.* New York: Oxford University Press, 1990.

Wendel, François. *Calvin: The Origins and Development of His Religious Thought.* Translated by Philip Mairet. London: William Collins Sons & Co., 1963.

West, W. M. S. "John Hooper and the Origins of Puritanism." Diss., Universität Zürich, 1955.

Wilcox, William George. "New England Covenant Theology: Its English Precursors and Early American Exponents." Diss., Duke University, 1959.

Wilder, Amos N. "The Puritan Heritage in American Culture." *Theology Today* 5 (1948): 22–33.

Williams, C. H. *William Tyndale.* London: Thomas Nelson & Sons, 1969.

Williams, J. Rodman. "The Covenant in Reformed Theology." *Austin Seminary Bulletin* 78 (1963): 24–38.

Wing, C. P. "Federal Theology." *Cyclopaedia of Biblical, Theological and Ecclesiastical Literature,* vol. 3 (1871), pp. 515–520.

Witherspoon, John. *The Works of John Witherspoon, D. D.* 9 vols. Edinburgh: Ogle & Aikman; J. Pillans & Sons; J. Ritchie; and J. Turnbull, 1804–1805.

Wolf, Erik. "Johannes Althusius." *The Encyclopedia of Philosophy,* vol. 1. New York, 1967.

Wolf, Hans Heinrich. *Die Einheit des Bundes: Das Verhältnis von Altem und Neuem Testament bei Calvin.* Beiträge zur Geschichte und Lehre der reformierten Kirche 10. Neukirchen-Vluyn: Neukirchener Verlag, 1958.

Yule, George. "Developments in English Puritanism in the Context of the Reformation." In *Studies in the Puritan Tradition: A Joint Supplement of the Congregational and Presbyterian Historical Societies,* pp. 8–27. Chelmsford, England: J. H. Clarke, 1964.

Zaret, David. *The Heavenly Contract: Ideology and Organization in Pre-Revolutionary Puritanism.* Chicago: University of Chicago Press, 1985.

Ziff, Larzer. "The Social Bond of Church Covenant." *American Quarterly* 10 (1958): 454–462.

———, ed. *John Cotton on the Churches of New England.* Cambridge, Mass.: Harvard University Press, 1968.

Zsindely, Endre. "Aus der Arbeit an der Bullinger-Edition: Zum Abendmahlsstreit zwischen Heinrich Bullinger und Johannes Burchard, 1525/1526." *Zwingliana* 13 (1972): 473–480.

Zuck, Lowell H. "Anabaptist Revolution Through the Covenant in Sixteenth Century Continental Protestantism." Diss., Yale University, 1956.

Indexes

Index of
Authors and Subjects

Index of
Scripture References

DATE DUE

FEB 1 7 2006			